ARISTOTLE'S
NICOMACHEAN ETHICS

Continuum Reader's Guides

Heidegger's Being and Time – William Blattner

Hobbes' Leviathan – Laurie Bagby

Hume's Enquiry Concerning Human Understanding – Alan Bailey and Dan O'Brien

Hume's Dialogues Concerning Natural Religion – Andrew Pyle

Nietzsche's Genealogy of Morals – Daniel Conway

Plato's Republic – Luke Purshouse

Wittgenstein's Tractatus Logico Philosophicus – Roger M.White

ARISTOTLE'S
NICOMACHEAN ETHICS
Reader's Guide

CHRISTOPHER WARNE

continuum

Continuum International Publishing Group
The Tower Building   80 Maiden Lane
11 York Road   Suite 704
London SE1 7NX   New York, NY 10038

www.continuuumbooks.com

British Library Cataloging-in-Publication Data
A catalogue record for this book is available from the British Library.

ISBN: 0 8264 8554 5 (hardback) 0 8264 8555 3 (paperback)

Library of Congress Cataloguing-in-Publication Data
A catalog record for this book is available from the Library of Congress.

Typeset by Servis Filmsetting Ltd, Manchester
Printed and bound in Great Britain by Ashford Colour Press Ltd,
Gosport, Hampshire

CONTENTS

PREFACE

This book discusses Aristotle's views about the best life for human beings as they are set out in his *Nicomachean Ethics*. Its aim is to introduce the reader to the principal themes and claims of the text by focusing on the arguments. In a book of this nature it is impossible to examine every issue and to go into as much depth as one would always like. This has meant on occasions that I have skated over some topics very briefly and have not touched on some others at all. However, I hope that what remains is of interest and of use.

There are many translations of the *NE* on the market today. W. D. Ross's has been a standard for many years and is still available from Oxford University Press. The most recent major edition, however, is that of Rowe and Broadie (2002). This is a monumental work and contains detailed historical and philosophical introductions together with extensive notes by Broadie. These notes are in some cases a more accessible guide to her views on the *NE* than can be found in her *Ethics with Aristotle* (1991). For the purposes of this commentary, however, I have selected Terence Irwin's translation (second edition) published by Hackett (1999). This is, I think, the most useful, affordable edition available. It too contains extensive notes and a very detailed glossary providing excellent advice on the usage of key Aristotelian terms. However, my use of this text should not be considered in any way a negative judgement about the quality of other translations and it is well worth consulting more than one English translation, particularly for difficult passages of the *NE*. All the references in this commentary give numbers of the Bekker edition (1831). I have used the abbreviation *NE* for *Nicomachean Ethics* and *EE* for the *Eudemian Ethics* throughout.

PREFACE

I have been helped in the writing of this book by Professor Nick Dent. My enthusiasm for the ideas discussed in the book originated in Nick's 'Greek Ethics' course at the University of Birmingham in 1997. He has patiently read the commentary and has given generously of his expertise in making suggestions that have greatly benefited the final text. Dr Andy Fisher and Mark Ellis read some early draft material and made numerous helpful suggestions. I am also grateful for the advice and encouragement of Professor Rob Hopkins, Dr Iain Law and Dr Chris Wraight. I have, furthermore, had the benefit of advice from Ian Price and Sarah Douglas at Continuum International Publishing. None of them, of course, bears any responsibility for any errors the book contains.

Although I have not acknowledged it at every turn, this text owes much to the scholarly and philosophical work of others. I have learnt much from the writing of Julia Annas, Sarah Broadie, David Bostock, Terence Irwin, Richard Wollheim and Michael Pakaluk. Even if their names do not appear throughout the text, this should not be taken as any lack of indebtedness.

It is a particular pleasure to be able to record in writing my thanks to my friends and family who have shown great support for me over the last couple of years. The friendship of Tom Humphrey has always been a blessing and no less so over the period of time in which I have composed this study guide. I am grateful for the personal support of Dr Andrew Teverson, Grant Gordon, Dr Saladin Meckled-Garcia, and Sam McIver. I owe thanks to Sarah and David Mitchell for welcoming me into their home in more difficult times. Finally and most importantly, I thank Christina Schultz. She has supported me at every point during the writing of this book.

Christopher Warne
Crystal Palace, London
21 January 2006

This book is dedicated to my parents,
Clare and Martin Warne, with love

CHAPTER 1

CONTEXT

In this section we will briefly consider Aristotle's life and works, considering in particular those texts that are pertinent to the present commentary. We will comment on their authenticity and their relationship to one another. We'll then examine Aristotle's stated methods for ethical inquiry and will assess how effective they are likely to be in generating results.

I ARISTOTLE'S LIFE

Aristotle was born in 384 BCE in Stagira, which was then part of Macedonia. It lies on the northeast coast of the peninsula Khalkidhiki, which is about 500 km north of Athens. Aristotle's father, Nicomachus, was physician to the court of King Amyntas II of Macedon and Aristotle's enduring interest in biology probably has its origins in his family's professional background. In 367 BCE, at the age of 17, Aristotle ventured south to Athens and entered Plato's Academy. He studied there for the next 20 years and Plato is reputed to have referred to him as the 'mind of the school'.

After Plato's death in 347 BCE Aristotle left Athens. The reasons for his departure are a subject of historical speculation. It has been suggested that Aristotle felt bitter at having been passed over to head the Academy: a position that went to Plato's nephew, Speusippus. However, he may equally have wanted to avoid the growing anti-Macedonian sentiment among Athenians. Philip II of Macedon, King Amyntas' son, was at that time carrying out his military ambitions in the south, which threatened Athens. The animosity felt towards those associated with his court would have placed Aristotle in a difficult position. Whatever his motivation, Aristotle moved to Assos where he married Pythias. After her death, some three years later, Aristotle moved to Mitylene with his female companion Herpyllis. Although they didn't wed, her place in his affections is clear to any reader of his will:

> the executors and Nicanor are to remember me in taking care of Herpyllis (for she was good to me) in all respects and in particular, if she wants to take a husband, they are to see to it that she is given away in a manner not unworthy of us . . . if she wishes to live in Chalcis, she is to have the guesthouse by the garden, if in Stagira the family house: whichever of these she wants, the executors are to furnish her with whatever seems proper to both of them and satisfactory to Herpyllis. (Diogenes Laertius, cited in *The Complete Works of Aristotle*, p. 2464)

In 343 BCE Philip II invited Aristotle to educate his son, Alexander (later, the Great). Aristotle accepted and, although little is known of the classes he delivered, several works addressed to Alexander have survived. He returned to Athens in 334 BCE and took out a lease on some buildings in the north of the city. These buildings housed his school, the Lyceum, where he conducted his research and teaching for the next 11 years. It was Aristotle's practice to spend his mornings walking about the school with colleagues and students discussing philosophical problems and solutions. It was in virtue of this practice of walking about that the academics working there were dubbed 'the Peripatetics' (literally, 'walking to and fro'). The Lyceum also had a terrific library: Aristotle amassed manuscripts, maps, samples and articles for illustration and study. This body of research materials was due partly to the patronage of Alexander.

Alexander himself died in 323 BCE and this again prompted a rise in anti-Macedonian feeling. Aristotle was charged with impiety and, unlike Socrates, fled because, he claimed, 'I will not allow the Athenians to wrong philosophy twice' (Vita Aristotelis Marciana Gigon, cited in *The Complete Works of Aristotle*, p. 2461). He returned to the region of his birth and died on the island of Euboea in 322 BCE from a digestive illness.

2

II ARISTOTLE'S WORKS

Aristotle's research was encyclopedic: he concerned himself with metaphysics, biology, physiology, astronomy, epistemology, logic and ethics. He published many treatises on these topics in his own lifetime, most of which, sadly, have been lost. However, a catalogue of these works has survived and it provides us with some indication of the diversity of his writing. The catalogue includes volumes entitled *On Memory*, *On Advice*, *On Pleasure*, *On Good Birth*, *On Olympic Victors*, *On Dissection* and *On the Dry*. It was on the basis of these published works that Aristotle was esteemed for the quality of his published prose: Cicero said of it that it was a 'river of gold' (*Academica* II xxxviii 119). This is perhaps not a quality that will readily strike his readership today. His texts can seem flat, terse and cryptic. Indeed, Arthur Schopenhauer thought that Aristotle's writing was best characterized as exhibiting a 'brilliant dryness' (1819 [1969], Vol. 1, p. 428). This feature of his writing undoubtedly owes much to the provenance of those works that survived. They are lecture notes – 'the most brilliant set of lecture notes ever written' (MacIntyre 1981 [2003], p. 147). Although they are brilliant notes, as working documents they do not always include clear references to other texts or state all the premises of arguments. While we can imagine that Aristotle would have expanded upon his notes when he delivered his lectures, as students of the *NE* today we need to be prepared to examine it carefully to identify his arguments, to uncover suppressed premises and to follow the progression of his ideas.

Of Aristotle's surviving works, there are four on ethical topics: the *NE*, the *EE*, the *Magna Moralia* and *On Virtues and Vices*. Although the authenticity of the first two works has not been seriously questioned, the attribution of the second two to Aristotle is generally thought to be spurious. One mystery, though, endures. Books V–VII of the *NE* are the same as Books IV–VI of the *EE* and are thus referred to as the 'common books'. The mystery concerns which work the common books originally belonged to, which in turn raises the matter of the chronology of the texts. Anthony Kenny has argued that *EE* is the later work, and that the common books belong to it, on the basis of computer analyses (1978). However, many commentators are of the view that *NE* represents Aristotle's later views and that the common books were carried over unrevised (see, for example, Bostock, p. 1). In this commentary we will examine the views expressed in the *NE*, which is still generally considered to express Aristotle's mature reflections on ethics, though we'll draw on the *EE* and on the *Rhetoric* (the latter containing useful popular descriptions of virtues, feelings and 'happiness') to elucidate some arguments and issues.

Before we continue it is worth dispelling one objection to the very reading of Aristotle's ethical works. The objection is that his moral views are not 'in tune' with ours. This objection is typically made with reference to his views that some people are natural slaves and that women aren't capable of deliberating with authority (*Politics* 1254a15–24 and 1260a13). The worry seems to be that if Aristotle thinks such things he can't be a very 'ethical' man and so we should ignore his views. This makes little sense: it would be like suggesting we shouldn't read *The Groundwork of the Metaphysics of Morals* because Kant thought that of the two sins, masturbation and suicide, suicide was less bad (*The Metaphysics of Morals*, p. 179). Aristotle's claims about slaves and women are certainly not implied by the arguments of the *NE* and so are not grounds to reject its ideas.

III   ARISTOTLE'S METHOD[1]

Two passages of the *NE* present us with statements of methodology. The first is at 1095a31–b12 and the second is at 1145b4–8. Neither passage is completely lucid; nor does Aristotle consistently adhere to the methods described in them. However, both passages merit our study and for two reasons. Firstly, at the very least, they provide us with an indication of Aristotle's approach in the *NE*, which can only aid our interpretation of the text and our grasp of its structure. Secondly, there are some very general questions about Aristotle's method in ethics that these passages may shed some light on. For example:

• How can we/should we philosophize about ethics?
• What kinds of insights can we expect Aristotle's methods to produce?
• What may we learn by the application of this method?

These are difficult questions and a full discussion of them is well beyond the scope of this book. There is, though, something to be gained through the consideration of such questions, even if we fail to answer them to our satisfaction: *viz* a better sense of the Aristotelian enterprise and of the status of its results. Let's begin by examining the two passages from the *NE*.

In the first, Aristotle comments that:

> We must notice . . . the difference between arguments from principles and arguments towards principles. For indeed Plato was right to be puzzled about this, when he used to ask if [the argument] set out from principles or led towards them – just as on a race course the path may go from the starting line to the far end, or back again. For we should certainly begin from things known, but things are known in two ways; for some are known to us, some known without qualification. Presumably, then, we ought to begin from the things known to us. That is why we need to have been brought up in fine habits if we are to be adequate students of fine and just things, and of political questions generally. (1095a31–b12)

Aristotle's thought here seems to be this: there is a distinction between arguing *to* and *from* 'principles'. The word 'principles' translates *'arche'*, which literally means 'starting point' or 'beginning' and, in the first two sentences cited above, it denotes the axioms – the most basic propositions or principles – of a discipline. We may, then, argue in one of two ways: either (i) argue from such axioms: that is, assume them true and arrive at new conclusions by inference from them; or (ii) argue to such axioms: that is, try to identify axioms by scrutinizing and seeking to explain and interpret a phenomenon. Aristotle recommends that in ethics we should argue in the second way. He then introduces a further distinction between 'things known': some things are 'known to us' and some are 'known without qualification'. The former refers to what is known according to human beings and the latter to what we would call necessary truths from which further truths can be inferred. Our arguments in ethics, Aristotle claims, must begin from what is 'known to us'. The relevant things 'known to us' are acquired through the good upbringing noted in the final sentence. So, in the *NE*, we argue to principles starting from what is known to us.

The second passage is slightly more accessible:

> As in the other cases, we must set out the appearances and first of all go through the puzzles. In this way we must prove the common

beliefs . . . ideally, all the common beliefs, but if not all, most of them, and the most important. For if the objections are solved and the common beliefs are left it will be an adequate proof. (1145b4–8)

We can distinguish three stages in this method: (1) the identification of 'appearances' (*phainomena*) that are expressed in common beliefs (*endoxa*) among which (2) there are problems and puzzles that are (3) to be resolved so as to preserve the common beliefs. So, we begin by gathering together the different views on a topic and note the tensions and contradictions between them. We then seek to resolve these tensions and contradictions to retain (presumably some of) the original views. The resolution of such contradictions is achieved by drawing distinctions, examining evidence and assessing the implications of these common beliefs. So, for example, in his discussion of the best life for human beings, Aristotle denies the 'appearance' that it is a life of pleasure (*NE* I.5), but later confirms that the best life will be pleasurable to the person who lives it (*NE* I.8) and thereby retains the 'common belief'. This confirmation is based on distinguishing the precise sense in which the best life is pleasant: it is not a life dedicated to the satisfaction of carnal pleasure, but is a life in which a person takes pleasure in doing what is right.[2]

The method described in this second passage is referred to as Aristotle's dialectic. While the aim of the method described in the first passage was the identification of principles, the aim of the dialectic is the preservation of common beliefs. Although common beliefs may be our 'starting point', the data from which we reason, there is no suggestion here that they constitute the principles that are the object of our inquiry. Furthermore, the dialectic seems, under the description given above, to have its limitations. Firstly, it's not clear why we should strive to preserve common beliefs as opposed to developing new ones. If we are minded merely to retain current beliefs we do not seem likely to make much 'progress'.[3] Secondly, and perhaps more worryingly, it's not obvious that the method will lead us to true propositions about the world. Nothing follows about the truth of the common beliefs we preserve from the process of making distinctions and so for to remove contradictions between them.

With regard to the first point, it should be remembered that Aristotle does *not* strictly adhere to the dialectical method throughout the *NE*. For example, in *NE* I.5 he seeks to identify the best kind of life for human beings and – consistent with the dialectic as described – starts by reviewing the views of the many and the wise. However, in *NE* I.7, Aristotle departs from the dialectic and argues for his own account of the best life without striving to resolve any contradictions between the views identified in *NE* I.5. So even if the dialectical method does limit us to the views people already have, it is not the only approach Aristotle deploys. But this line of thought is unlikely to satisfy those who think the deployment of the dialectic is methodologically conservative. To such critics, we may note that the process of resolving tensions and contradiction between the common beliefs involves making distinctions that may constitute some kind of progress. As we saw above, Aristotle's distinction between different senses of 'pleasure' resulted in a new view about the sense in which the best life is pleasurable.

With regard to the second point, it seems correct that the dialectical method does not necessarily generate true propositions about the world. It would be unfair, though, to suggest Aristotle was unaware of this. In the *Topics* he clearly states that 'for the purposes of philosophy we must treat [propositions] according to their truth, but for dialectic only with a view to opinion' (105a30–31). Furthermore, it should not be thought that Aristotle intends to take seriously *every* point of view on a phenomenon. In the *EE* he restricts the range of opinions or views he'll take into account, setting aside the views of children, sick people and the insane (*EE* 1215b30). What remains are the reputable opinions, and to this extent Irwin's translation of '*endoxa*' as 'common beliefs' is slightly misleading. Aristotle is not suggesting we seek to resolve tensions between every point of view, but only those that are reputable. But, reputable or otherwise, even the views that remain may contain falsities and this does constitute a constraint on the dialectic.

To the extent that we follow the dialectic *strictly* we can expect results that present us with one way of rendering consistent the reputable views we have about the best life and good action. This is, though, subject to the qualification that there may well be other such consistent ways of making sense of the reputable opinions from which we began. So although the dialectic does not lead to the truth and, in fairness, does not pretend to, it does provide us with *a* means of making sense of the apparent phenomena concerning the best way to live. It is to be admitted, then, that any conclusions we reach are highly qualified, but we may end this examination of Aristotle's methodology on a more optimistic note.

First, Aristotle's methods strive for *positive* results and to this extent they may be contrasted with the Socratic method of *elenchus*: Socrates is represented as proceeding by questioning the views of others and thereby exposing their views as incoherent. As a result, the early Platonic dialogues characteristically end in *aporia* (literally, an impasse) and do not expound a positive theory. Aristotle's methods, however, seek positive outcomes through the resolution of incoherence and the identification of principles. The achievement of such resolution involves recognition of the puzzles exposed through *elenchus*. But Aristotle tries to go beyond these puzzles to settle on a view that does justice to the reputable views we have.

Secondly, given the subject matter, we may wonder whether a better method could be envisaged. It's noteworthy that psychologists working today in the field of the 'science of happiness' base their arguments on the results of questionnaires in which people self-assess their happiness or well-being.[4] Consider the following statement of methodology: 'We shall rely to a large extent on the subjective reports of how people feel: if people say they're happy then they *are* happy . . . Subjective reports do not, however, always agree with ratings made by other people or with objective measures. We shall regard such findings as problems to be explained' (Argyle, p. 2). I won't point out the strong parallels between this passage and 1145b4–8. But we should stress that Aristotle's method is seemingly no worse than some contemporary work in psychology that takes as its privileged data first-person reports about emotions, feelings and moods.

CHAPTER 2

OVERVIEW OF THEMES

In this section we will consider approaches to studying the *NE* with a view to our engaging with it in the most satisfying and effective way. This will take us fairly quickly to the question the *NE* may be read as addressing and which I'll refer to as 'Aristotle's question'. We will then run through some of the major themes of the work, noting some of the main interpretative issues those themes evoke.

I STUDYING THE *NE*

Jonathan Barnes remarks, in his introduction to the Penguin edition of the *NE*, that he will not attempt to 'extol the merits of the *Ethics*: a good wine needs no bush; and it is mere impertinence to advertise the rarest of vintages' (p. 10). There is much truth in this, but the merits of the *NE* are not always immediately obvious to new readers, recognition coming through sustained, reflective engagement. Such engagement can sometimes seem laborious and the experience of early frustrations can be dispiriting. It is, then, worthwhile considering how we might study the text most profitably.

Many readers are likely to encounter the *NE* at university on courses on philosophy, classics or the history of ideas. Such courses often require students to complete assessed essays and, given the pressures on time, some may be tempted to establish quickly Aristotle's point on a certain matter and to accumulate a list of the objections that show him to have been wrong. The identification and evaluation of objections is, of course, a vital part of the philosophical enterprise, but their value is limited if one has little or no sense of the goal of an author's work. If philosophy is reduced to the statement of an author's view followed by a statement of its falsity, it is perhaps inevitable that it will assume the character of an irrelevant intellectual pastime that makes no connection with a life being lived: a dismal conclusion to one's efforts.

Karl Popper always stressed that we are better able to grasp a philosopher's work by reading it as addressing certain questions and problems that have significance for us all and thereby merit our concern and engagement. This might suggest that a satisfying reading of a philosophical work requires a simple list of the questions the philosopher hopes to answer. And indeed, the reader will find in the present commentary lists of study questions at the end of each section. But mere awareness of such a list does not by itself put us in a position fully to appreciate a philosophical work. We need to share in the problems and questions for ourselves; see them as having force and moment in our lives; and to recognize them as urgent and pressing. In approaching a text in this way, we go far beyond the identification of 'who said what' and witness some of the greatest minds actively seeking solutions to problems whose true complexity we more fully appreciate. There is no more stimulating and energizing an intellectual encounter available when reading great works of philosophy.

Our task, then, is to scrutinize the questions that motivate the *NE* and, as a result, to gain a better appreciation of their significance and of what hinges on their resolution. In the case of the *NE* this process is perhaps easier than in other areas of philosophy. It's not always obvious, for example, why people get quite so worked up about theories of naming. By contrast the *NE* speaks to questions about the nature of a life well lived, which are, I take it, of enduring significance. Popular works about living happy or successful lives are prominently on display in 'all good bookshops' and promise recipes for the achievement of such lives. To speak loosely, we all make decisions about what to do everyday: we want them to be good decisions that we don't regret; we don't want to 'waste our time'. Since the *NE* addresses these issues, there are perhaps more points of continuity between the *NE* and our everyday lives than, for example, in certain areas of metaphysics. We must, though, probe a little deeper.

II ARISTOTLE'S QUESTION

The question that drives the *NE* is 'What is the supreme or best good for human beings?' Superficially, this question doesn't appear to have much, if any, force for people who aren't interested in achieving or acquiring the 'best good', whatever that amounts to. It seems a question one could quite happily ignore while getting on with the everyday business of living. The suspicion that Aristotle's question is practically irrelevant for some people may be fuelled by the title of the work: *The Ethics*. Such a title connotes notions of rightness and wrongness, moral goodness, duty and obligation. And isn't it just *obvious* that there are very many people who ostensibly aren't interested in the prescriptions of morality, are wholly self-absorbed and are apparently untouched by human suffering? So if the 'supreme good' is analysed as the 'morally good', Aristotle's question is relevant only to those who want to be 'morally good'.

The line of thought outlined above is confused. To start with, although the title of the text is *The Ethics*, this is a transliteration of the Greek *'ta ethika'*, which literally means 'Of character'. Now a treatise on character does not obviously connote notions of moral goodness, duty and obligation; and I will stress throughout this commentary that it would be a mistake to *assume* from the outset that Aristotle is concerned with what we think of as morality. This is not to say that the text is not concerned with morality as we conceive of it, just that we should not *assume* it is on the basis of the English rendering of its title. However, even if the *NE* is not a work of moral philosophy, it remains true that Aristotle's question only has significance for those people who want the 'supreme good'.

Perhaps, then, we should consider the substance of the supreme good in the *NE* and see whether it is something that everyone actually wants. Aristotle thinks the supreme good for human beings is 'happiness': living and acting well. If this is the supreme good, then Aristotle's question has significance, at least, for those who are interested in living such lives. But we can still imagine people for whom such a notion seems lofty and irrelevant to the 'real' decisions of life. After all, worrying about the constitution of human happiness is seemingly distant from the business of getting the kids up, fed and to school before heading off to work oneself.

I think we can better grasp the significance of Aristotle's question by examining the formal nature of the supreme good. Aristotle thinks it trivially true that all our actions aim at some good. What he means by this is that when a person *acts* he does so with a view to achieving some goal that is, in his estimation, important, valuable and worth doing. This is true both of a gangster 'rubbing out' an unfaithful associate and of a charity worker distributing aid to the victims of a natural disaster. Both have identified some goal they deem important and valuable; and through their actions they try to achieve that goal. There are, then, as many goods as there are goals in human action and on this account sustenance, shelter, entertainment and the esteem of others are rightly reckoned human goods because they are goals we seek to realize. We have, then, the notion of a good: what of the *supreme* good?

The supreme good is formally defined as that good which we seek only for its own sake and for the sake of which we seek everything else (1094a18–20; 1102a2–3). This definition implies a relationship between the goods we seek. Some goods are sought for the sake of other goods; some goods are sought just for themselves. We might, for example, produce bridles and saddles for the sake of riding horses. The riding of horses is the good, or goal, that explains why we bother to produce bridles and saddles at all. We can equally imagine some goods that we seek just for themselves; perhaps listening to a piece of music or going for a walk. We want to go for a walk because it is refreshing or invigorating and not for the sake of some further goal. It may be thought, though, that 'refreshment' and 'invigoration' represent further goals to which 'going for a walk' is merely an instrument. This is, of course, quite possible: a person may have his heart set on refreshment and accept *any* available means of procuring it. But it seems equally possible that a person may want 'the refreshment of going for a walk' (goal) as opposed to 'refreshment' (goal) achieved (in this case) by 'going for a walk'. For Aristotle, the goods we want for their own sake are those that we judge to be appealing, valuable or worthwhile and which we do not seek as instruments to further goods. We are now in a position to make sense of the concept of the supreme good: (i) it is that good, or goal, we seek for its own sake and not as an instrument to some further end; (ii) it is that good, or goal, for whose sake we ultimately do everything else we do. To sum it up, the supreme good is that good in which all our desires come to rest.

One implication of the supreme good, so defined, is that it is the ultimate source of value in our lives. The goodness or value of anything hinges decisively on its standing in the correct relationship to the supreme good. So, Aristotle's question is really concerned with the identification of that goal in human life that is the ultimate basis of all our actions. The possibility of our performing any meaningful actions in life depends on our achieving the supreme good: without it all our desires would be 'empty and futile' (1094a22). It follows, then, that anyone who wants to make meaningful decisions and perform purposeful actions has an interest in considering the nature of the supreme good. As Aristotle comments, a person 'should set up for himself some object for the good life to aim at . . . with reference to which he will then do all his acts, since not to have one's life organized in view of some end is a mark of much folly' (*EE* 1214b8–11). The point here is that a person who has not thought about and reflected upon the ultimate end in life may 'waste his time' pursuing one goal and then another more or less willy-nilly without a thought as to the relative importance of such goals in the context of his whole life. It is, of course, true that a person may unthinkingly give precedence to a certain good or may merely accept without reflection the goals of his family or friends. But to the extent that he does so, he fails to achieve the supreme good, which requires deliberation about the ends, and consideration of their proper importance, in life.

III THEMES AND ISSUES OF THE *NE*

In this section we will introduce the principal themes of the *NE* and some of their attendant issues. The intention is to prepare the reader both with regard to the content of the text and the main controversies surrounding its interpretation. The discussion does not pretend to be comprehensive, but hopefully it will be sufficient to represent Aristotle's thought in its critical context.

Aristotle thinks the supreme good for human beings is *eudaimonia*, which is traditionally translated 'happiness'. The notion was in common usage long before Aristotle wrote the *NE* and literally means 'sweet angel' (*eu* = sweet and *daimon* = angel). A person who achieves *eudaimonia* is one whose life is blessed by such an angel. Aristotle does not attend to the term's etymology and uses it synonymously with living and acting well. In this commentary, I will leave the Greek term untranslated, so it may be useful to set out its different word classes. A person may be said to live a *eudaimon* (adjective) life, that is, a life in which he lives and acts well. We may refer to him as a *eudaimon* (adjective) person because he lives a *eudaimon* life. And we may again, abstracting somewhat, refer to what the person has: *eudaimonia* (noun). The primary conception here seems to be that of a *eudaimon* life because our most basic grasp of the matter under discussion is of a life well lived. The other word classes derive from this most basic sense: we look at a person's life and, if it is excellent, say the person is *eudaimon*.

One of Aristotle's principal projects is to analyse a *eudaimon* life: to identify its nature and components and what control, if any, we have over securing it. To this end, he surveys and rejects various popular analyses – a life of carnal pleasure, for example – and proceeds to argue for his own conception by examining the function of human beings. The function of a thing is its characteristic activity or what it typically does: so, the function of a baker, for example, is to bake things and a *good* baker carries out that activity well. In this Aristotle was undoubtedly influenced by Plato who deployed the notion of 'function' to argue that human excellence consists in the control and activity of the mind (*Republic* 352d–354b). Aristotle, though, draws a different conclusion: a person has a *eudaimon* life if throughout it he possesses and exercises the virtues.

One of the main controversies in the interpretation of the *NE* concerns the nature of a *eudaimon* life as Aristotle characterizes this. There are, on the one hand, those who think *eudaimonia* is a 'dominant end' and, on the other, those who think it an 'inclusive' end. Those who think it a dominant end claim that there is just one activity that is constitutive of a *eudaimon* life; a view that Aristotle's remarks in *NE* X about the 'life of contemplation' certainly encourage. There, he appears to claim that we should dedicate as much time as possible in life to the contemplation of knowledge. But to other commentators, this view is incredible and they claim that a *eudaimon* life comprises a range of (good) activities and is thus an *inclusive* end. We have, then, a divisive point of interpretation. Where does this leave us? Well, in our engagement with the *NE*, we should consider whether the alleged controversy is well founded or whether it is based on a misunderstanding of the relevant texts. If it is well founded we must consider how it can be resolved. Its resolution is not just a scholarly matter: it is central to our own efforts to make sense of the notion of *eudaimonia*.

Having analysed a *eudaimon* life as a life throughout which a person exercises the virtues, Aristotle begins an examination of the virtues. In general the virtues of a thing are relative to its function: they are those characteristics that make it good and carry out its function well. So, for example, the virtues of a doctor may include accuracy in diagnosis and sensitivity to a patient's feelings because these are among the characteristics that make a doctor good *as a doctor*. They are, furthermore, those characteristics that make him carry out his function well: they enable him to treat patients' ailments effectively and relieve them of suffering. This conception of virtue differs substantially from the popular conception of a virtuous person as a kind of moral saint selflessly dedicated to the well-being of others, perhaps even to the detriment of his own.

Aristotle claims that human virtue comprises both virtues of character and virtues of thought. The virtues of character are states or dispositions that make a person well off with regard to feelings and desires. For example, a brave person is 'well off' with regard to fear because he feels it only when the circumstances merit it; conversely a coward is 'badly off' with regard to fear because he conceives of everything as fearful and consequently experiences fear more frequently than is right. Aristotle defines virtues as 'intermediate states': those that fall between two opposing extreme states, which he labels vices. The virtue of thought operative in virtue of character is practical wisdom. Practical wisdom is that ability of ours to judge correctly, all things considered, the best action to perform in any given situation. So, the brave person exercises practical wisdom because he correctly conceives of his circumstances as meriting fear and judges correctly how to respond. The coward, however, fails to exercise practical wisdom and so conceives of an unthreatening situation as dangerous.

Any account of virtue is controversial. To some minds, talk of virtue is hopelessly antiquated and has no real bearing on the lives we live today. What matters to us is the rightness and wrongness of action; or what we have a duty to do or a duty not to do. Virtue, if indeed any such thing exists, is very much on the sidelines. What makes matters worse in Aristotle's case is that the virtues he identifies seem to be primarily concerned with the well-being of the person who has them. So even if virtue is not an outdated notion, in Aristotle's hands it is distastefully individualistic and certainly not something we would try to develop in our children as he recommends. But against this, there are those who claim the notion of virtue is far from otiose. We continue to describe people as 'just', 'generous' and 'kind' and when we do so we commend them. The notion of virtue illuminates the nature of these commendable characteristics. Furthermore, Aristotle explicitly claims that the virtuous person acts for the sake of what is fine and not for his own sake, which conflicts with the claim that a *eudaimon* life is peculiarly self-absorbed.

One of Aristotle's contentious claims is that people are responsible for the states of character they possess. So, a virtuous person is to be praised for his excellent character and a vicious person blamed for his deplorable character. The argument for this conclusion appears in Aristotle's wider discussion of voluntary and involuntary action. He argues that character is a product of repeated actions: if those actions were voluntarily performed, the resultant state of character is voluntarily acquired too. This strikes some commentators as unpalatable: surely in some cases, at least, a person's vicious character is not (entirely) voluntarily acquired. He may have been the victim of abusive carers or have been set a poor example. According to some, Aristotle stubbornly insists the person had a choice and his state of character remains partially, but crucially, 'down to him'.

Since complete virtue is hard to achieve and consequently rare, it seems inevitable that many people will fall short of it. But even if this is true, it doesn't follow that the many who fall short are vicious. Between the extreme cases of virtue and vice, Aristotle plots two further conditions of character that are perhaps more frequently realized: *enkrateia*, or strength of will, and *akrasia*, or weakness of will. The enkratic person does what the virtuous person would do, but not without having to struggle to control his desire to do something else. The akratic person judges correctly the best thing to do, but, unlike the enkratic person, fails to control his desire to do otherwise and as a result acts on his desire and not his better judgement. What puzzles philosophers here is how a person who does what is wrong can be appropriately described as knowing what is right. The question seems especially difficult because Aristotle claims that in every action we aim at something we judge to be good.

The final theme I will note here is that of friendship. Aristotle clearly thinks friends are part of a *eudaimon* life and Books VIII and IX contain some of the most illuminating of all the discussions of the *NE*. Aristotle is concerned to discriminate the varieties of friendship, in particular the variety proper to a *eudaimon* life; and to clarify the relationship between being friends and being *eudaimon*. The discussion also raises issues that are pertinent to our understanding of the virtuous person. To give just one example: does the beneficent person act for the sake of another or for the sake of himself? Aristotle's remarks on this question illuminate the true motivation of the virtuous and the pleasure they take in active life.

These then are the principal themes of the *NE* that we should bear in mind as we work through the text. The commentary follows the sequence of Aristotle's text and generally includes remarks about each chapter. In some cases, however, chapters are passed over. This is not because they are of no interest or value; it is just because some central matters merit more detailed examination in an introductory text of this nature.

CHAPTER 3

READING THE TEXT

I *NE* I

Introduction

Aristotle's principal concern in *NE* I is to identify and analyse the supreme good for human beings. We have already noted that the supreme good is the ultimate goal or end of a human life. But what could the ultimate goal be? Superficially it seems difficult to think that there will be just one answer: if we ask people, friends and family what they ultimately seek in life we are likely to receive a wide range of responses. One person's ultimate goal is world renown; another's a Maserati MC12. Aristotle is well aware of the plurality of ends in life and of the diversity of opinion as to the supreme good (1097a15–23; 1095a20–5). Much of this diversity is due to the specific interests of individual human beings. A Picasso lover may work extremely hard in the hope of one day owning an original canvas. But there is no pretending that everyone will have this as a goal, still less an ultimate goal. Aristotle's concern is to identify the ultimate goal of human beings as a *natural kind*. As such his discussion is conducted at a certain level of generality. In this connection it's worth noting Aquinas' remark on this very issue: 'even if [the] general starting points allow of no exceptions, the more we get down to the particulars the more exceptions occur' (*Summa Theologiae* 1.94.4). The point is not that there is a more precise account of *eudaimonia* available but one that currently lies beyond our powers of inquiry. Rather, the point is that at a certain level of specificity there is no precise account to be had.

The structure of *NE* I may not be immediately apparent to new readers and so it may benefit them to have a sketch of its contents before we begin:

- *NE* I.1–2: Arguments (apparently) for the existence of the supreme good.
- *NE* I.3: How much precision we should expect in our inquiry; what the students must already know.
- *NE* I.4: Agreement about the name of the supreme good; disagreement about its substance.
- *NE* I.5–6: Popular and academic views of the supreme good.
- *NE* I.7: Aristotle's conception of the supreme good (the function argument).
- *NE* I.8: How Aristotle's view coheres with popular views; place of external goods.
- *NE* I.9–11: The cause of the supreme good; the role of fortune.
- *NE* 1.12: The supreme good is not praised, but blessed.
- *NE* 1.13: The parts of the soul; introduction to the virtues.

It is not always clear how these different topics follow on from one another so I will throughout try to emphasize the connections as we examine the chapters.

I.1–2
We have already noted that Aristotle thinks the supreme good is a human goal or end. This is confirmed in the first sentence of the *NE*: 'Every craft and every line of inquiry, and likewise every action and decision, seems to seek some good; that is why some people were right to describe the good as what everything seeks' (1094a1–3). Some commentators have argued that this short passage contains the following argument for the existence of the supreme good:

(i) Every action and decision aims at some good.
∴
(ii) There is some (particular) good at which all actions and decisions ultimately aim.

The problem with this inference is that it's invalid: the premise can be true and the conclusion false without contradiction. This can be seen from the analogous invalid inference below:

(i*)   All roads lead to somewhere.

∴

(ii*) There is somewhere – e.g. Rome – to which all roads lead.[5]

It seems, then, that Aristotle, the father of logic, begins the *NE* with a logical howler. But this, of course, *assumes* that he infers (ii) from (i) and that assumption is false. It's not even clear that Aristotle regards (ii) as true at *this* stage in his inquiry: at 1097a23–4 he claims that 'if there is some end of everything achievable in action, the [supreme] good . . . will be this end; if *there are more ends than one*, [the good achievable in action] will be these ends'. If Aristotle thought he had proved there is just one good at which we ultimately aim, why would he concede a few chapters later that there might be more than one? It seems to me that Aristotle is making conceptual points in this opening passage: (1) anything that is an action will have some aim that is, in the agent's estimation, good, valuable or worthwhile; and (2) the (supreme) good is the aim of all human actions.

In *NE* I.2 Aristotle offers the following definition of the supreme good:

> Suppose then that the things achievable in action have some end that we wish for because of itself, and because of which we wish for the other things, and that we do not choose everything because of something else – for if we do, it will go on without limit, so the desire will prove to be empty and futile. Clearly this end will be the good, that is to say the supreme good (1094a18–22).

The supreme good, then, is that good or goal that we seek for its own sake and for the sake of which we seek everything else. There are some things I may seek as *instruments* to further ends. A person may try to get a job, for example, solely as an instrument for procuring money. If an alternative means for procuring money presented itself – e.g. a lottery win – he may no longer seek employment. The supreme good, however, is not sought as an instrument to some further end: it is sought because of its own intrinsically appealing characteristics. Furthermore, it is for the sake of achieving the supreme good that we undertake *all* the other actions we perform in life. However, this passage has been interpreted as another proof for the existence of the supreme good:

(1) If there is something we want for its own sake and not for the sake of something else, then it will be the supreme good.
(2) If we want everything for the sake of something else, then our desires will ultimately be empty and futile.
[(3) Our desires are not ultimately empty and futile.]
∴
[(4) There is something we want for its own sake and not for the sake of something else.]
∴
[(5) There is a supreme good.]

This interpretation is unconvincing: to begin with (3), (4) and (5) are not stated in the passage. But even if these are implicit, the most that Aristotle could claim to have shown is that there is *at least* one good that we seek for its own sake and not the stronger claim that there is *only* one such good. Bernard Williams has suggested the passage can just as easily be read as specifying the consequence of there not being a supreme good rather than as a proof of its existence. But anyway, as he himself remarks, 'the passage is . . . confusedly expressed and it is perhaps impossible to say exactly what it means' (1962, p. 292).

The third argument that Aristotle is alleged to adduce infers the existence of the supreme good on the grounds that there is a highest discipline (political science) and that the object of political science is the procurement of the supreme goods for the citizens of that community of people (1094a28–1094b11). But once again the argument seems flawed for it is not clear that political science does aim at the procurement of the supreme good for its citizens: Western states prescribe laws that seek the protection of peoples. So what are we to take away from these first two chapters?

It seem that if we assume *NE* I.1–2 is intended to prove the existence of the supreme good, we must conclude that it fails. However, I would resist the assumption. Aristotle was lecturing to an audience that would have been familiar with the notion of the supreme good. He refers at 1094a2 to the principle that *the* good is the goal sought by everything, which he later attributes at 1172b10–17 to Plato's pupil Eudoxus. So it doesn't seem to me that Aristotle takes himself to be introducing to philosophy a *new* concept that he has to argue for. Rather he is spelling out what kind of an end he takes the supreme good to be and identifies it with the end of political activity.

1.3

Having stated that his inquiry aims to identify the supreme good for human beings, Aristotle tells us we shouldn't expect too much precision in research into practical matters (1094b13–15). This is because practical disciplines depend on the particular facts of the matter (Broadie 1991, p. 19). Consequently generalizations like 'money is good' are practically imprecise: in some situations money is good, but in others it's not (1129b2–5; cf. *Meno* 87e–88c). Aristotle's point is that we must be sensitive to the nature of our subject matter and should not expect results that are more precise than is possible. It's worth noting, though, that Aristotle does not mean the study of ethics is necessarily imprecise (Bostock, p. 6); only insofar as the study of ethics is *practical* does it admit of such imprecision.

Secondly, Aristotle's claims that young people are not in a position to benefit from the study of ethics because they lack 'experience of . . . actions in life, which are the subject and premises of our arguments' (1095a2). Although Aristotle's concern is to make us good, he doesn't think that listening to his arguments is sufficient for bringing that about (cf. 1179b5–6). To understand those arguments we must have shared in the sorts of experiences he refers to and that means we need to have been (fairly) well brought up.

I.4

In *NE* I.4 Aristotle begins his inquiry into the nature of the supreme good. There is, he claims, general agreement as to its name: it is *eudaimonia*, which is typically translated as 'happiness' (1095a19). There are, however, differences between the concept 'happiness' and '*eudaimonia*'. Firstly, we tend to think of happiness as a psychological state, roughly that of having a positive attitude or feeling towards some object in the world. I'm happy, for example, that my son passed his exams. But according to Aristotle, *eudaimonia* is not a state; it's an activity, it's something we *do* (1098a16). Secondly, we tend to think that people can't be mistaken about whether they're happy or not, but, as we shall see, people can be mistaken about whether their lives are *eudaimon*. And thirdly, we think of happiness as something transitory. I was happy last night that Ronnie won the snooker, but I am miserable now that I have to work. *Eudaimonia*, however, is not transitory; it applies to one's whole life. So, a person can't be *eudaimon* one minute and not the next (1098a19).[6]

However we do need some sense of *eudaimonia* before examining Aristotle's account of it. When he first introduces the term, Aristotle claims that it is synonymous with 'doing and living well' (1095a20). This is perfectly consistent with his earlier claims about the concept of the supreme good. The supreme good, remember, is that which we want for its own sake and for the sake of which we want everything else. If we consider the ultimate goal in human life, intuitively we think it is to live well and successfully.

Despite the general agreement about the name of the supreme good, there is considerable disagreement regarding its substance (1095a20). Some people think *eudaimonia* is money or pleasure; others think it is honour or esteem. In fact, Aristotle points out, some people's conception of *eudaimonia* changes with their circumstances: when they're poor, they think it's money; when ill, they think it's health (1095a24–5). Aristotle doesn't intend to consider all these views. Instead, he proposes an examination of the most popular accounts that seem to be supported by argument (1095a29–31). In *NE* I.5–6 Aristotle considers and rejects various substantive accounts of *eudaimonia* and it is to these that we now turn.

I.5

Aristotle considers the so-called 'lives' of pleasure seeking, honour, contemplation and money making. His aim is to see whether any of these goods or ends could intelligibly be the *ultimate* goal of all our actions. Is it the case, for example, that we do everything for the sake of pleasure? He rejects the accounts he considers here, except the 'life of contemplation', which he examines in *NE* X. When studying this section it's important to keep in mind that Aristotle doesn't think that pleasure and money making, for example, are without value, still less that they're not *components* of the best life. He is merely trying to ascertain whether any of these could be the *supreme* end.

The masses, Aristotle claims, identify *eudaimonia* with pleasure (1095b18–19). He dismisses this analysis, claiming that such a life is fit for grazing animals (1095b20–1). The comparison with livestock makes reasonably clear that Aristotle has in mind a life whose ultimate goal is carnal gratification: a life spent trying to satisfy bodily desires for food, drink, sleep and sex. Although he doesn't *argue* that this life is not *eudaimon* (though cf. *NE* VII.12 and X.2), it's worth noting we don't even think the satisfaction of some bodily desires is good, let alone the *supreme* good. Think of the satisfaction of the desires of the heroin addict or the glutton. So despite not having an argument here, we do have a prima facie case for thinking *eudaimonia* is not a life of carnal pleasure.

Aristotle claims that more 'cultivated' people identify *eudaimonia* with honour or esteem (1095b22–4). For such people, the achievement of the esteem or recognition of their peers is the ultimate goal of their actions. However, Aristotle thinks such people are mistaken. Firstly, honour seems to depend more on those who confer it than those upon whom it is conferred. *Eudaimonia*, though, is 'something of our own'; it is something that depends on what *we* do (1095b26). Secondly, Aristotle claims that people only want to be honoured to convince themselves that they're good. If this is true, honour can't be the supreme good because the supreme good is something we want for its own sake and not for the sake of something else.

Perhaps, then, *eudaimonia* consists in being good or virtuous (1095b33–5). However, the mere possession of virtue is consistent with one's suffering grave misfortunes or prolonged unconsciousness, which 'no one would consider *eudaimon*' (1096a1–2; cf. 1153b19).[7] So, a person is not *eudaimon* because he possesses virtue. Finally, Aristotle disqualifies the 'life' of money making because money is only an instrumental good and so straightforwardly fails to satisfy the conception of the supreme good in *NE* I.2.

I.6

Aristotle then turns to Plato's 'Form of the Good'. His treatment of Plato's view is dense and technical; consequently it's rather inaccessible to readers approaching the text for the first time. Since Aristotle's own account doesn't hinge on the arguments here, readers may want to ignore this chapter initially and return to it later. My intention is only to provide a very brief introduction to Aristotle's comments. Readers wanting to examine the arguments and ideas in more depth should follow the references in the notes.[8]

In Platonic metaphysics the objects of the world are instantiations of what he called 'Forms' or 'Ideas'. Plato thought that Forms were exemplars that exist outside space and time and of which secular objects are inferior instances. So, when we say 'this is a trowel and that's a trowel too', we're saying both objects stand in the appropriate relation to the Form of 'trowel'. As Aristotle puts it they have 'one character common to many individuals' (*Metaphysics* 1079a3–4). Plato thought that there was a Form of the Good and it follows that all those things that are good stand in the appropriate relation to the Form. As Aristotle interprets Plato, everything that's good must have some common property and it's this claim that Aristotle denies.

Aristotle's rejection of the Form of the Good is based on a series of technical arguments (1096a17–1097a14). I will comment on the argument at 1096a24–9:

(a) If there is a Form of the Good, the predicate 'good' will denote a single property.
(b) But 'good' denotes different properties in different categories: in substance 'good' denotes mind or God; in quantity 'good' denotes the right amount.
(c) 'Mind', 'God' and 'the right amount' share no common property.
∴
(d) There is no Form of the Good.

However, Aristotle seems to have misinterpreted Plato here. Plato could argue that although 'mind' and 'the right amount' have many differing properties, they nonetheless share the property of 'being exemplary of their kinds'. This would render (c) false and the argument unsound. In fact, Aristotle himself conceives of goodness as relative to a thing's kind.

I.7

In this chapter Aristotle argues for his own substantive account of *eudaimonia*. He begins by introducing some constraints on the concept '*eudaimonia*' (1097a15–b21). He then argues for his own account that satisfies these constraints (1097b22–1098a21). The purpose of the initial conceptual analysis is to clarify what 'supremacy' amounts to when we talk of the supreme good. Such clarification will make us better able to determine whether anything actually answers to the concept.

Aristotle claims that *eudaimonia* is (1) the 'most complete end' (1097a30) and (2) is 'self-sufficient' (1097b8). To say these are conceptual constraints is just to say that they're qualifications of what is meant by the term *'eudaimonia'*. In introducing them, Aristotle is not making a claim about the substance of *eudaimonia*. He is merely indicating what kind of an end *eudaimonia* is: something that is necessary because of the plurality of ends in life (1097a15–22). An end is 'complete' if we want it for its own sake (1097a31). As Aristotle points out, there are very many ends in life, among which we can discriminate those ends that are instrumental from those that are not (1097a26–27). Take, for example, making a donation to a shelter for the homeless. If I make the donation for the sake of the further end of achieving an estimable reputation, then my donation is merely instrumental and so not complete. However, if I make the donation simply for its own sake, because I think it the best thing to do with my money, it is complete. Aristotle claims that the 'most complete end' is sought *always* for its own sake and *never* for the sake of anything else (1097a29–33).

An end is 'self-sufficient' if, by itself, it makes a kind of life 'choiceworthy' and 'lacking in nothing' (1097b15). By this, Aristotle means that *eudaimonia* cannot be improved by the addition of any other good (b17–19). This claim is controversial. If, implausibly, we interpret Aristotle as claiming that *eudaimonia* can't be improved because it incorporates everything that is good, it's obviously false because none of us can have *everything* that is good. However, if, more plausibly, we interpret Aristotle as claiming that *eudaimonia* incorporates a range of goods, but certainly not *all* goods, its title to unimprovability is jeopardized. Suppose you have enough wealth to look after your family, make donations to shelters and have fantastic holidays three times a year. That may sound like a pretty good life: but wouldn't it be even better if you had a bit more money and could go on more holidays or help more shelter projects?

At 1097b7 Aristotle claims that the completeness constraint follows from the self-sufficiency constraint. The point is this. If it's false that *eudaimonia* is self-sufficient, then it's false that it's complete. For if there was an end that was in some sense superior to *eudaimonia* (rendering *eudaimonia* not self-sufficient), we would pursue *eudaimonia* not only for its own sake, but also for the sake of that superior end (so *eudaimonia* would not be complete). It is important to bear this point in mind when considering whether Aristotle's substantial account of *eudaimonia* satisfies these constraints: if it's self-sufficient it will automatically be complete.

At 1097b22 Aristotle begins his substantive account of *eudaimonia*. He suggests that we can determine the nature of *eudaimonia* by examining the 'function' (*ergon*) of human beings (b25). This brings us to what is known as the 'function argument'. This argument has generated a voluminous secondary literature, all the avenues of which I don't intend to explore here. Let's start with the argument itself, which appears at 1097b25–1098a20, and an interpretation of its premises and conclusion.

(i) X is good if X performs its 'function' well (1097b25–9).
(ii) Human beings have a 'function' (1097b31).
(iii) The distinctive 'function' of human beings is the activity of the part of the soul that has reason, which comprises both the part with reason and the part obedient to it (1098a3–5).
∴
(iv) A good human being exercises the part of the soul with reason well or excellently throughout a complete life (1098a14–15).

Aristotle supports the principle expressed in premise (i) by analogy with crafts (*techne*). The 'function' of a flute player is to play the flute; a good flute player is one who performs that 'function' well or excellently (1097b26–9). Although the principle doesn't imply, as some readers of a book on ethics might expect, that a thing that performs its 'function' well is *morally good* – for a good flute player may nonetheless be a rogue – the principle certainly has some intuitive appeal. However, there is another interpretation of the passage 1097b25–9. On this account the principle is that the 'function' of X is good for X if that 'function' is performed well. On this interpretation, playing the flute well is good for the flautist as a flautist. The confusion derives from the phrase *to anthropinon agathon*, which can be interpreted both as 'human goodness' and as 'good for humans' (Bostock, p. 26; cf. Whiting *passim*). However, Aristotle evidently thinks that to do what is good for humans is to be a good human, though we're perhaps more sceptical about such a connection.

Premise (ii) strikes the modern eye as rather controversial for two reasons. Firstly, some commentators interpret (ii) as the claim that human beings are instruments designed for some purpose. Such an interpretation may be appealing in religious contexts, but outside them it's far from intuitive. Secondly, Aristotle appears to argue invalidly from the claim that the organs of the body have 'functions' to the conclusion that human beings have a 'function' (1097b32–4). However, even if the organs of the body have some 'function' it doesn't follow that human being do too. Matters here can, I think, be clarified to some extent by examination of what is meant by 'function'.

The Greek word is *ergon*. Although this is typically translated as 'function', a better, though more cumbersome, translation is 'characteristic way of life'. To understand what this means we must consider Aristotle's conception of the soul (*psyche*).[9] The first point to note is that Aristotle doesn't think souls are distinctive to human beings: all living things have a soul. The second point is that something's soul is determined by its form (*eidos*). By 'form' Aristotle has in mind the way that any particular organism is structured: a geranium is structured one way, a human being another. One consequence of the differences in structure is a difference in capability. For example, geraniums are capable of extracting nutrients from soil, but aren't capable of engaging in conversation. The relationship between a thing's soul and its *ergon* is to be understood in terms of the characteristic behaviour of that thing given its capabilities. So, the *ergon*, or characteristic activity, of the flautist is to play the flute and the *ergon* of the eye is to see.

Understood in this way, we can reject the 'instrumental' reading of premise (ii) because an organism can have a characteristic activity without being designed for some further purpose. It's also clear that Aristotle need not *infer* that human beings have an *ergon* on the ground that the organs of the body have an *ergon*. The human being has an *ergon* because it is a living being with a distinctive form and consequently a distinctive range of capabilities. However, what is far from clear is that, given the range of human capabilities, there is *an* activity characteristic of human beings. After all, human life seems to comprise a very wide range of activities: cooking, eating, dancing, writing, stealing and so on. This, then, brings us to premise (iii): the claim that the characteristic activity of human beings is the activity of the part of the soul with reason.

Aristotle argues for (iii) on the ground that the activity of the part of the soul with reason is distinctive to human beings. He identifies three parts of the soul: nutrition and growth; sense perception; and reasoning. Aristotle claims that the activity of extracting nutrition from the environment is shared with plants and so is not the distinctive *ergon* of human beings (1098a1). He argues that the activity of perception is shared with animals and so is not the distinctive *ergon* of human beings (a2). By a process of elimination, then, Aristotle infers that the human *ergon* is the activity of the part of the soul with reason. Unhelpfully, the only immediate clarification of this claim is Aristotle's remark that the part of the soul with reason comprises both the part that 'obeys' reason and the part that has reason itself (a3–4). This remark is clarified to a degree in Chapter 13, and I will comment on it more fully when I deal with this. For now, though, we should note that this is the part of the soul that is involved in feeling, desire and thought. The part responsible for feelings and desires 'obeys' the part responsible for thought.

Nagel objects to Aristotle's reasoning here. He claims that the activity of the part of the soul with reason is *not* distinctive to human beings: it is shared with the gods (Nagel, p. 10; cf. 1178a22–3). However, he argues that Aristotle is nonetheless right to privilege the part of the soul that reasons over the parts responsible for nutrition and perception. This is on the ground that these other parts of the soul are in the service of reason. Reason, however, is not exclusively in the service of those parts of the soul (ibid, p. 11). What is distinctive about human life is that it is directed by the exercise of the part of the soul with reason: human beings act for reasons and not merely on 'instinct'. So, it is true that human life comprises a wide variety of activities none of which seems more distinctively human than others. Aristotle's point, though, is that rational activity itself is what is distinctive of human kind.

Aristotle's conclusion (iv) is that a person is *eudaimon* if, throughout his life, he exercises the part of the soul with reason excellently. Stated thus, the conclusion seems disappointing. However, by examining some of the complaints hereabouts we can, I think, go some way to appeasing Aristotle's opponents.

One quite natural complaint is that the conclusion is vague. Aristotle himself, however, only regards (iv) as a 'sketch' of *eudaimonia* (1098a22). And there is, I think, good reason for this: recall his remark from *NE* I.3 that we should not expect more precision than the subject matter allows (1098a27–8). We can, though, make a bit more sense of the conclusion. The word translated 'well' or 'excellently' in (iv) is *arete*. This is elsewhere translated as 'virtue'. The conclusion can then be read as an activity of the part of the soul with reason in accordance with virtue or, more simply, a life of virtuous activity. But, what is such a life like? Does such a life satisfy the conceptual constraints identified in the first part of *NE* I.7?

To take the first question, the character of the life of virtue is really the topic of the rest of the *NE*. However, I think we can make some general comments here. It is a life that is shaped and directed through the exercise of virtue. The exercise of virtue is involved both in the actions that make up that life and the overall destination of it. This is sometimes referred to as the 'life plan' interpretation of *eudaimonia*. Although Aristotle never explicitly refers to such a plan, it is clear that the exercise of virtue implies it (see, for example, *NE* VI.5) for the virtuous person decides on the best things to do and the determination of that must refer to some conception of a whole life.

However, does Aristotle think that the activities, and goods, of a life shaped by virtue are partly constitutive of *eudaimonia* or does he think that the exercise of virtue by itself is constitutive of *eudaimonia*? This brings us to the question of whether Aristotle's account is Inclusive or Dominant (or Exclusive). The terminology derives from Hardie (p. 23). An Inclusive end is one that incorporates two or more goods. A Dominant end is constituted by just one good. The issue is that different passages of the *NE* support contrasting interpretations of what *eudaimonia* consists in: Aristotle's remarks in Book I seem to support an Inclusive account whereas the remarks in Book X seem to support a Dominant account. I will not review all the relevant passages here and will comment on this issue more fully in my discussion of Book X.[10]

Aristotle claims that *eudaimonia* 'needs external goods': wealth, friends and so on (1099a34–b6). One way of interpreting this is as a kind of conjunction. The *eudaimon* life is equivalent to the conjunction of the exercise of virtue, the possession of money, friendships and so on. I think this interpretation is wrong. We have been given no independent account of the source of the value of these other goods. The alternative appears to be to claim that these other goods are merely necessary for the virtuous activity that is constitutive of *eudaimonia*. But on this account external goods are not valuable in their own right, which seems to conflict with our intuitions.

I think the solution can be discerned from Aristotle's comment in Book V that these are goods that are 'good . . . without qualification, but for this or that person not always good' (1129b3–4). The point being that money, for example, is good, but that it is only good if it is correctly managed in the context of a whole life. Cooper usefully introduces the terminology of first- and second-order goods at this point (pp. 96–7). First-order goods are those specific things we actually want such as money, holidays, friendships and so on. *Eudaimonia* is not a first-order good: we don't want money, holidays, friendships and, additionally, a *eudaimon* life. Rather it is a second-order good that consists in the 'attempt to put into effect an orderly scheme for the attainment of these first-order ends' (ibid.). On this reading, virtuous activity is what is responsible for the correct management of external goods into the *eudaimon* life. We can now see the sense in which *eudaimonia* is unimprovable. If we interpret Aristotle as claiming that *eudaimonia* is a first-order good, the claim that no life is unimprovable seems pertinent. For we can readily imagine that the addition of any extra first-order good would improve the existing conjunction. However, if we interpret Aristotle as claiming that *eudaimonia* is a second-order good, the objection seems wide of its mark. For the activity of correctly ordering all the goods available to one in life cannot be improved by the addition of an extra first-order good: it can only be improved by more excellent management. But since, *ex hypothesi*, *eudaimonia* is the best, it implies that that management is already excellent and so is unimprovable.

The second question above was whether the conclusion (iv) satisfies the conceptual constraints Aristotle developed in the first part of the chapter. The conclusion does state that the *eudaimon* life is 'complete' but it's clear that this is not the sense of 'complete' Aristotle introduced at the beginning of Chapter 7 for it refers to the exercise of virtue throughout one's life rather than its status as desired only for its own sake. So, Aristotle must think that the life of virtuous activity is desired only for its own sake. To some extent, the comments above go towards substantiating that claim. However, it still seems that the life is not the one most people have in mind when they think of the best life we can live. Aristotle tries to address this complaint in his discussion in Chapter 8.

I.8

Aristotle thinks that his account of *eudaimonia* should accord with the everyday intuitions people have about it (1098b9–10). These are the intuitions that surfaced in the popular accounts of *eudaimonia* in *NE* I.5. Aristotle claims that 'it is reasonable for each group not to be completely wrong, but to be correct on one point at least, or even on most points' (1098b27–8). To this end he tries to demonstrate that the account in *NE* I.7 reflects the intuitions that motivate the popular accounts in *NE* I.5. However, the discussion here does much to resolve the worry that the account in *NE* I.7 is not in its sketched form 'complete'.

Aristotle first considers the life of virtue, which he rejected at 1095b32–3. He states here that the account in *NE* I.7 accords with the intuition that the 'best life' involves virtue in some way. However, he stresses here the difference between possession and exercise of virtue. He claims that it's necessary for us to 'act and act well' (1099a4). This, then, constitutes a modification to the view expressed in *NE* I.5.

At 1095b18–22, Aristotle rejected the identification of pleasure with *eudaimonia*: to organize one's life around the pursuit of pleasure is not the best kind of life. Aristotle claims here that the *eudaimon* life will be pleasant, but only with certain qualifications (1099a6). It is a commonplace that different things please different people and not every kind of pleasure will be found in the *eudaimon* life (a12). However, the *eudaimon* life is lived in accordance with virtue (1098a17) and, as we shall see in our examination of Book II, Aristotle thinks that the proper exercise of the virtues is pleasurable. So, it's true that *eudaimonia* is pleasurable, but false that the aim of that life is the maximization of carnal pleasures.

I.9–11

Having specified the sense in which his account of *eudaimonia* is consistent with popular views, Aristotle considers the cause of *eudaimon* lives. Is it acquired through learning or habituation? Or is it bestowed by God or a matter of good fortune? Aristotle thinks that we become *eudaimon* through learning and habituation. However, he also recognizes that fortune has some role to play. After all, we might be reluctant to say that a person whose life was cut short by a chance injury lived the best sort of life. Aristotle discusses the role of fortune in *NE* I.10–11. He asks whether we can count a person as *eudaimon* in his own lifetime or whether we should follow Solon's advice and 'look to the end' (1100a10–11). His point being that if fortune has some role to play in our living *eudaimon* lives, we won't be able to rule out a reversal in our fortunes until our lives are over. So it seems that ascriptions of *eudaimonia* can never be safely made until after a person's death (1100a17).

However, this point conflicts with the intuition that we ought to be able to count someone as *eudaimon* while he is alive and flourishing (1100a34–5).

Aristotle first identifies the intuition that lies behind Solon's dictum. Our reluctance to count a person as *eudaimon* owes to the possibility of his fortunes changing in his life. Imagine, for example, a person who is flourishing but who is involved in a serious car accident that renders him paralysed and incapable of looking after himself. Even if we were tempted to count him as *eudaimon* before the accident, we are unlikely to do so afterwards because *eudaimonia* is stable throughout one's life.

In response to this Aristotle claims that a person's fortunes don't determine his *eudaimonia* (1100b8–10). What controls his *eudaimonia* is the performance of virtuous activities (1100b10–11). Since the virtues are taken to be stable states of one's character, the *eudaimon* person will exercise virtue throughout his life (1100b18–22). So it is acceptable to call a person *eudaimon* during his life if he has virtuous states of character. But it's important to note that there are limits. Aristotle concedes that there are blows that may befall a person who has a virtuous character from which it will take a considerable time to recover (1101a10–13). Even so, a *eudaimon* person will never be 'miserable' because a miserable person does what is hateful and base (1100b34–5).[11]

I.12

Having identified the role of fortune in the acquisition of a *eudaimon* life, Aristotle considers whether *eudaimonia* is something to be praised or prized. He argues that *eudaimonia* does not fit the logical structure of praise: 'Whatever is praiseworthy appears to be praised for its character and its state in relation to something' (1101a13–14). Aristotle's point is that when I praise something I do so with reference to something else. For example, the distance Sam throws a javelin may be praiseworthy because it exceeds the distance thrown by everyone else. We refer to the distance thrown by everyone else when we judge how successful or otherwise Sam's throw was.

Aristotle claims that *eudaimonia*, however, cannot be praised. This is because there would have to be something else with reference to which we could judge the greatness of *eudaimonia*. But this is not possible because *eudaimonia* is the best thing a human being can achieve. In this respect Aristotle considers the absurdity of praising gods. The gods are perfect and so we may judge some other thing's greatness with reference to them. However, we cannot praise the gods themselves because that would imply there being something greater than the gods with reference to which we could judge them. Aristotle concludes, then, that *eudaimonia* is something to be prized and not praised.

NE I.12 is the end of Book I. The final chapter introduces the virtues.

I.13

The nature of the virtues occupies the next five books of the *NE*. As I indicated in relation to Chapter 7, Aristotle's account of the *eudaimon* life is based on his remarks about the nature of the soul. In Chapter 13 Aristotle comments on the part of the soul that has reason, because it's the excellent activity of this part of the soul that's constitutive of the *eudaimonia*.

The soul can be distinguished into a rational and non-rational part. These parts are distinguished by their respective functions and so it does not matter whether they are distinguished as parts of the body or by nature (1102a30–2). The non-rational part can be further resolved into a part that is responsible for nourishment and growth and a part that 'shares in reason' (1102b15). The part that 'shares in' and 'listens to reason' is the part with feelings and desires. The virtues of character belong to this part of the soul. The virtues of thought, which are related to the virtues of character, belong to the part of the soul that has reason. Although there is much of interest in this section I will restrict my comments to the sense in which the non-rational soul listens to the rational soul. This is of central importance to an understanding of the relationship between the virtues of character and the virtues of thought.

Aristotle thinks it clear that the part of the soul that is responsible for growth cannot be influenced by reason. Reason is impotent with regard to growth: reason will not make us, for example, taller, by which I mean that reasoning is not causally effective in matters of growth. However, reason and thought do play a role in that part of the soul that is responsible for feelings and desires. This can be demonstrated with an example.

Imagine that you're not vegetarian and that I offer you a hamburger from the barbecue. You start eating the burger and savour its delicious flavour. Whatever else we might say about you, we can say that you have a positive attitude towards the burger and that partly on the basis of this attitude you continue eating the burger. Now imagine that I inform you that what you are eating is in fact minced rats; we may fairly assume that your attitude towards the burger will change. It will be a source of revulsion and this revulsion might be expressed in your spitting out the contents of your mouth.

The point of this fiction is to show the extent to which one's feelings and desires 'listen to reason'. For what has certainly not changed in the example is the burger. You're eating the same meat. However, your beliefs about the burger have changed: at first you thought it was beef, after I intervened you believed it was rat. Since you believe, for the sake of argument, that rat is putrid or disgusting, your attitude towards the burger changed. Your once positive attitude towards it became negative. And it was this change in attitude that shaped your desire to spit the burger out.

The sense in which one part of the soul 'listens to reason' is just this: reason is drawn upon in our grasping the situation we're in. That is to say our feelings, and our desires, depend upon what David Wiggins calls 'situational appreciation' (1975–6, p. 233). The attitude we take towards a situation depends upon our understanding of our situation and on some judgement of ours as to the value of aspects of that situation. It is important to note how strong the contrast here is with Hume. Hume thought that reason was inert and a mere slave to the passions (*Treatise* II, iii, 3). On Hume's account a person's desires are independent of reason. For Aristotle, feelings and desires are intimately related to the exercise of reason. Our feelings are not arbitrary, but are determined by the importance we assign to some aspect of ourselves and of the world. If I judge the consumption of rat at a barbecue to be disgusting, then I will be repulsed by the burger I'm eating when I learn of its contents.

Summary

So, Aristotle has begun his inquiry arguing that we must identify the nature of the best life for human beings. He has framed this in terms of our goal or aim in life. He rejects certain candidates for the ultimate goal and argues for his own account by examining the human function. This revealed that our ultimate goal is a certain way of life that is defined by the exercise of the part of the soul possessing reason. Aristotle thinks that this way of life is something largely within our control, though he concedes that fortune makes a contribution to some extent. Finally he has suggested that the nature of the *eudaimon* life is such that it is not to be praised but prized because it doesn't fit the logical structure of praise. In *NE* II Aristotle begins his analysis of the virtues.

Study questions

1. What is the relationship between the supreme good and the living of worthwhile lives?
2. Does Aristotle give persuasive reasons for thinking the supreme goal in life is not the enjoyment of pleasure?
3. Is Aristotle's use of the concept of function successful?
4. Why is Aristotle concerned with the question whether a person can be called *eudaimon* in his own lifetime?
5. Is Aristotle's account of the relationship between thoughts, feelings and desires convincing?

NE II

Introduction

Aristotle has argued that *eudaimonia* is an activity of the part of the soul that has reason in accordance with virtue throughout a whole life (1098a16–20). We have taken this to refer to a life that is shaped and directed by the exercise of the virtues. Now, as Aristotle has acknowledged, the details of his account of *eudaimonia* need to be filled in (1098a22–3). The discussion of the virtues in *NE* II–VI fills in some of those details. For Aristotle, virtue comprises both the virtues of character and the virtues of thought (1103a15): he examines the virtues of character in *NE* II and the virtues of thought in *NE* VI. Although these virtues are *theoretically* separable, we shall see that, in Aristotle's view, the possession and exercise of either of them requires the possession and proper coordinated exercise of them both.

It will be profitable at this point to recall what Aristotle means by 'virtue of character' (*ethike arete*). Thomson misleadingly translates the expression 'moral virtue': although some Aristotelian virtues of character, for example justice, have what we might call a 'moral dimension', others, for example wittiness, do not. A person's failure to be witty is not obviously a *moral* failing, if it's a blameworthy failing at all. So, the scope of *ethike arete* is wider than that of moral virtue.

What, then, are the virtues of character? In general, the Greek word 'arete' is one of the most 'powerful words of commendation used of a person' (Adkins, p. 31). Socrates identified virtue with knowledge (see, for example, Meno 87D–89A). Aristotle disagrees: he thinks the virtues of character are those laudable traits that cause a person to be good and to carry out his function well (1106a17–18). We might, for example, admire a person's readiness to help others in need or his equitable resolution of conflict or his generous hospitality. Correspondingly there are traits of a person's character we may deplore, viz vices. We might, for example, deplore a person's obsessive desire to be the centre of attention or his insensitivity to others' needs or his tendency to 'fly off the handle' without notice.

Aristotle's aim in NE II is to specify the nature of the virtues of character. To do this he compares and contrasts virtues with skills or crafts (techne). The comparison is a useful one: both virtues and skills are relatively stable features of a person and both enable a person to do certain sorts of thing. For example, a trained steeplejack is able to fix chimneys and a just person is able to distribute wealth fairly. Despite these similarities, Aristotle argues that virtues are importantly different from skills (see also NE VI.4). In identifying these differences, the nature of virtue is further clarified.

II.1

Aristotle begins his discussion by considering how the virtues of character are acquired. He claims that they are habituated (1103a18), by which he means that a 'state [of character] results from [the repetition of] similar activities' (b21–2). This is one of the respects in which virtues are similar to skills: one acquires the ability to play the flute by practising playing the flute and one becomes just by performing just actions. So, Aristotle's first claim is: (V1) a virtue is a habituated state of character.

Although virtues are habituated, there are two reasons why it would be a mistake to regard them as habits. Firstly, as von Wright notes, habits are action-specific (p. 143). The habit of tapping one's foot, for example, is always manifested in that action. The virtues, by contrast, do not denote specific actions: one can display temperance by eating a slice of chocolate cake or, on another occasion, declining a slice of chocolate cake. Secondly, the term 'habit' sometimes suggests that the agent performs the action without thinking about it. One may, for example, be in the habit of putting one trouser leg on before the other without having the thought 'Now, right leg first' in mind before one does so. Such behaviour is sometimes characterized as 'mindless' for precisely this reason. The point is, though, that the virtues are not 'mindless'. A person only acts virtuously if he knows what he is doing and decides to do it (1105a32). So, virtues are habituated states of character, but are not themselves habits.

Aristotle argues for his account of the origins of virtue by rejecting two alternative accounts: (a) virtues are 'by nature' or innate and (b) virtues are taught (1103a16; a19–20; cf. *Meno* 99E). He argues against (a) on the ground that what is innate cannot be brought into another condition through habituation. A person who is congenitally hard of hearing, for example, cannot be made to hear better by any process of habituation. However, a person can become more generous through a process of habituation and so Aristotle concludes that virtues are not innate. One objection to this line of thought is the idea that people have innate characteristics. We're apt to describe a child as brave, for example, who doesn't 'break down' when in pain or in danger. This raises the issue of 'natural virtue', a problematic phenomenon that Aristotle addresses in *NE* VI. For now, let's simply note this apparent counterexample.

Aristotle doesn't argue against (b) in this chapter. This is disappointing, particularly because (b) appears to conflict with the reasonably strong intuition that we *are* taught 'good behaviour' by our guardians. As children we may have been told to share with others and to honour invitations we have accepted even if a more attractive option arises later. If we grow up to be the kind of people who share with others and honour invitations, we might be tempted to think that we were taught to do so because we were so instructed. Although we can concede that children are told that this, that and the other is right or wrong, the question is whether this amounts to their being 'taught'.

Burnyeat notes that Aristotle thinks habituation constitutes a way of learning distinct from induction, perception and so on which represent alternative ways of learning (pp. 72–3; 1099b9–11). A person who becomes generous through a process of habituation, for example, has learnt what generosity is in what Burnyeat calls a *strong*, as opposed to a *weak*, sense. To learn what generosity is in the weak sense is to learn the piece of information that 'generosity involves correctly giving of one's wealth'. To learn what generosity is in the strong sense, however, is to have repeatedly performed generous actions and through their performance come to appreciate what generosity is and what is attractive about it (p. 76). Burnyeat, then, suggests that a person is generous only if he has learnt what generosity is in the strong sense. Therefore, there is a distinctive kind of learning necessary for the possession of virtue, and habituation is precisely that kind of learning. On Burnyeat's account, being told that this and that are virtuous does not amount to our being 'taught' virtue in the strong sense. We can only achieve that through the performance of virtuous actions (cf. 1105b10–12).

II.2

Aristotle has claimed, then, that virtues of character are habituated through the repeated performance of virtuous actions: our states of character are controlled by the actions we perform (1103b30–2). We need, then, an examination of the nature of virtuous actions, which the rest of *NE* II is dedicated to. Aristotle makes three preliminary points.

The first is that right actions accord with 'correct reason' (*orthos logos*) (1103b33). This claim surfaces again at 1107a1–3 but is only properly discussed in *NE* VI. We'll say nothing more about it here. Aristotle's second point concerns the degree of specificity we should aim to achieve in our account of virtuous actions. In *NE* I.3 he stated that we should not expect more precision than the subject matter allows. His second point here is that the account we should expect of particular actions is even 'more inexact' than the general account of practical matters (1104a7–8; cf. 1094b23–1095a2). A navigator, for example, may have some general principles, but his application of them depends upon the nature of the situation he finds himself in. And a person's ability to know what general principle to apply in what situation requires some kind of insight (Joachim, p. 75). It's worth pointing out that Aristotle does *not* think there are principles or rules for action and that acting virtuously consists in applying such principles.

Aristotle's third point is that virtues of character are states 'naturally ruined by excess and deficiency . . . for if . . . someone is afraid of everything, stands firm against nothing, he becomes cowardly; if he is afraid of nothing at all . . . he becomes rash (1104a13–22). The references to 'excess' and 'deficiency' anticipate Aristotle's discussion of the 'doctrine of the mean' in *NE* II.6. The explicit purpose of the doctrine is to distinguish virtuous states from vicious ones.

II.3

Aristotle thinks that virtuous states of character are habituated by taking pleasure in the right things and being pained by the wrong things (1104b10ff.). So, I become generous by taking pleasure in giving appropriately and by finding stinginess unpleasant. However, *NE* II.3 begins with the claim that 'we must take someone's pain or pleasure following his action to be a sign of his state . . . if [someone] stands firm against terrifying situations and enjoys it, or at least does not find it painful, he is brave' (1104b5–10). This suggests that pleasure and pain are not merely causally necessary for the acquisition of virtue but are constituents of the acquired state when it is exercised.[12] If we read Aristotle in this way we can take him as specifying the following necessary condition for the possession of virtue: (V2) a person *P* possesses virtue *V* only if *P* takes pleasure, or is at least not pained, in performing actions expressive of *V*. According to this definition a person who gives money to a worthy cause but only with great reluctance is not generous. This is not to say, of course, that such a person does something bad. Aristotle characterizes such people as *enkratic* or self-controlled and, although they do not exhibit virtue, they certainly merit praise for doing what is good.

One obvious objection to (V2) is that it seems false: acting in accordance with virtue is not always pleasurable and so acting with pleasure cannot be a necessary condition of acting virtuously. Think, for example, of the temperate person who declines a second helping of tiramisu: such a person forgoes the pleasure of that second helping. However, the objection misses the point. Aristotle is not claiming that virtuous actions are pleasurable in the sense that the performance of them produces exclusively agreeable sensations. He's claiming that when one acts virtuously, one acts gladly and without reluctance: the performance of the virtuous action is not something that conflicts with the virtuous person's preferences. It is, in fact, an *expression* of his preferences and it's possible for a person to perform an action that is, in one respect, painful, which is nonetheless an expression of his sincere preference.

In his examination of courage, Aristotle explicitly addresses this issue. 'It is not true, then, that in the case of every virtue its active exercise is pleasant; it is only pleasant insofar as we attain the end' (1117b6). And further, 'for boxers find the end they aim at, the crown and the honour, pleasant – but being flesh and blood . . .

they find it painful to bear punches' (1117b3–5). This is a clear acknowledgement that the performance of virtuous actions might be painful. However, Aristotle doesn't think this falsifies (V2): what makes a painful action pleasant is the *fineness* of the end the virtuous person aims at. The virtuous person acts with pleasure because he acts for the sake of 'the fine' (*kalon*). This characteristic of virtue does not appear in the definition of virtue at 1107a1–3. However, as we shall see, 'for the sake of the fine' is perhaps *the* common feature of the virtues. It will be worth pausing to consider the nature of 'the fine' before we continue because it is a central (and a difficult) notion in Aristotle's account of the virtues.

Although the fine, the pleasant and the expedient are identified as ends worthy of choice at 1104b31, nowhere in the *NE* does Aristotle provide an analysis of 'acting for the sake of the fine'. The fine is contrasted with the shameful (1104b34) which is something confirmed in the *Rhetoric*: 'those actions are fine for which the reward is simply honour, or honour more than money . . . fine also are those actions whose advantage is enjoyed after death' (1366b36–1367a2; cf. 1390a2). Fine actions, then, are admirable and noble. So we may say tentatively that 'acting for the sake of the fine' means something like acting for the sake of what is admirable, noble or right. However, even if this is correct we face two further problems: firstly, it seems implausible to claim that the psychological content of a person acting virtuously includes reference to the fine; secondly, Aristotle has claimed that we ultimately act for the sake of *eudaimonia* and not the fine.

With regard to the first problem, Aristotle doesn't think that the virtuous agent has the thought 'I will do *x* because that is the fine thing to do' in mind when he acts. It makes more sense here to read 'acting for the sake of the fine' as defining a set of (admirable or noble) reasons that are the typical reasons for acting virtuously. For example, I may help a person *because he is in need* or I may put myself between my wife and her assailant *because she's in danger*, where the reasons 'because he's in need' and 'because she's in danger' are admirable or noble reasons for acting. A person then acts for the sake of the fine if he acts for reasons typical of the virtuous person.[13]

With regard to the second problem, it's worth recalling the relationship between virtue and *eudaimonia*. Aristotle has claimed that a person lives a *eudaimon* life if he possesses and exercises the virtues throughout his life (*NE* I.7). As we shall see, he also claims that what makes something good and able to perform its function well is its being virtuous (*NE* II.6). We have just learnt that a person acts virtuously if he acts for the sake of the fine. So, putting these claims together we can see that a person has a *eudaimon* life if he acts virtuously and he only acts virtuously if he acts for the sake of the fine. So, Aristotle thinks that a person is virtuous if he performs virtuous actions with pleasure. As we have interpreted him, he means that a person gladly does what is fine even if that involves enduring some pain. Aristotle presents a series of arguments for this claim and although we shan't consider them all, we will examine his argument at 1104b14–18:

(1) Virtues are concerned with actions and feelings.
(2) Actions and feelings imply pleasure or pain.
∴
(3) Virtues are concerned with pleasure and pain.

The first point to note, here, is that (3) is not equivalent to (V2). The conclusion (3) states only that there is some relationship between virtue, pleasure and pain, but not that virtue is related to pleasure in the way specified by (V2). The second point to note is that (2) seems obviously false: not *all* actions imply pleasure or pain. Combing one's hair, for example, or applying deodorant are apparently neither pleasurable nor painful. However, if we interpret (2) in the sense that we perform every action either willingly or reluctantly it appears more credible (cf. the interpretation of (V2) above). Nonetheless, even if (2) can be interpreted in some way such that it is true, (1) and (2) do not entail (3) (Hutchinson, p. 84). This can be seen if we compare the argument to the structurally analogous one below:

(1*) Aesthetics is concerned with works of art.
(2*) All works of art have a price.
∴
(3*) Aesthetics is concerned with prices (ibid.).

We could deny (3*) and assert (1*) and (2*) without contradiction and so this argument is invalid. Hutchinson comments that 'even as [a] weak argument for the claim that virtues have to do with pleasure and pain [it's] unconvincing' (ibid.). However, let's proceed on the basis that Aristotle's conclusion is true even if this particular argument, at least, is poor.

We may nonetheless question the significance of (V2). For does it really matter to us whether the person who helps us does so gladly or reluctantly? For (V2) could be true, but nonetheless be irrelevant to our appreciation of one another's actions. This objection is particularly relevant for those who want virtue to constitute the foundation of a normative ethical theory. Now, there are certainly conspicuous differences between the virtuous person and the *enkrates*. The virtuous person wants to act in the right way; the *enkrates*, in one sense at least, does not and may resent doing what frustrates his preferences for something else. So, acting correctly will certainly be *easier*, less of a chore, for the virtuous person than the *enkrates* because there is no conflict in his soul. But is this an important or significant difference?

To the extent that actions performed with or without pleasure imply judgements about what the agent considers valuable or worthwhile, I think the difference between the virtuous person and the *enkrates* is a significant one. There is a sense in which the *enkrates* doesn't judge the right action to be, all things considered, the best thing for him to do at that time. He has a strong inclination to do something else. As we said in our discussion of *NE* I.13, (some) desires are dependent on our judgements about what is good (worthwhile) or bad (pointless). So for a person, who is aware of all the relevant particulars, to continue having strong desires to do something other than what he judges the best action, implies his judging that something else as good. Now, I take it that a person's feelings and judgements in action are, sometimes at least, significant to us. The person who begrudgingly saves my life judges in a sense that my life is not worth saving. The truth of this is captured brilliantly in an example in Rousseau's *The Reveries of a Solitary Walker*: 'In all the ills that befall us, we are more concerned by the intention than the result. A tile that falls off a roof may injure us more seriously, but it will not wound us so deeply as a stone thrown deliberately by a malevolent hand. The blow may miss, but the intention always strikes home' (p. 128).

II.4

A puzzle seems to arise from the claim that one acquires virtue through doing what is virtuous. Imagine someone who thinks that doing what is virtuous is a sufficient condition for possession of virtue. If that's true then one couldn't *acquire* virtue through doing what is virtuous because in doing what is virtuous one *exercises* virtue (which obviously implies possession) (1105a17–21). In support of his case, the opponent might claim that a person who produces sentences of grammatical English possesses knowledge of English grammar. Aristotle rejects the claim that doing what is virtuous is sufficient for possession of virtue. He begins by denying his opponent's claim is true even in the 'grammar case'. It is, he claims, perfectly possible to produce grammatical sentences by chance (1105a23). We only attribute knowledge of English grammar to a person who produces sentences of grammatical English *because of* his understanding of grammar (1105a24–5). Aristotle goes on to note a more general and significant disanalogy between skill and virtue (1105a26). The products of skill are judged excellent on the basis of their own qualities (1105a29), but the same is not true of virtue. For an action to be virtuous, it is not sufficient that it accords with what is right; it must also be an expression of the right state of a person's character (1105a32). Aristotle states this difference in the following claim: (V3): an agent acts from a virtuous state if (i) he knows what he is doing; (ii) he decides on his action and for its own sake; and (iii) he performs his action from a firm and stable state of character (1105a32–5).

Aristotle points out that although (i) is true of both virtue and craft, it is the least significant of the conditions for virtue (1105b1–4). The interpretation of (ii) is controversial, but for our purposes we can read (ii) as the claim that the virtuous person acts for the sake of the fine and not for any other reason.[14] Condition (iii), however, is rather controversial.[15] For why should Aristotle think that a person only acts virtuously if he acts from a permanent state of character? Hutchinson thinks that the falsity of (iii) entails the falsity of (ii) (p. 105). He claims that one can only decide to do what is virtuous for the sake of the fine, and not for any other reason, if one has become a lover of virtue (ibid.). And a person can only become a lover of virtue if one has habituated a virtuous state of character (pp. 105–6). On this interpretation a person's possession of virtue guarantees his acting for the 'correct reason'; a person who does not possess virtue may act for a variety of reasons, not all of which are laudable. Think, for example, of a person who adheres to the speed limit but only to avoid paying a penalty.

We are now in a position to understand Aristotle's resolution of the puzzle. The opponent argued that doing what is virtuous is a sufficient condition for possession of virtue. Aristotle's characterization of the state of the virtuous person demonstrates that this claim is false. One can perform an action that, in similar circumstances, a virtuous person would perform, without being in the same state that the virtuous person would be in. And a central case of this, again, is the *enkrates*, which we have discussed above.

II.5

Aristotle argues that virtue is a species of the genus 'states of character': (V4) a virtue is a state of character. He has already insinuated this claim into his discussion at a number of points (1103b21; 1104a12; 1104b6; 1105b31). In *NE* II.5, though, he argues for it. The structure of the argument is quite straightforward:

(A) Virtues are either feelings, capacities or states (1105b20–1).
(B) Virtues are not feelings (b30).
(C) Virtues are not capacities (1106a8).
∴
(D) Virtues must be states (a13).

Aristotle begins by explaining what he means in (A) by feelings, capacities and states. By 'feelings' Aristotle includes both emotions, such as fear, confidence and love, and appetites or desire. This is unusual, from a modern perspective, because we tend to think that there is a formal distinction between emotions and desires. For example, strong cognitivists argue that emotions are cognitive states and as such necessarily involve a belief, whereas desires do not. We needn't get caught up in this matter of classification here because nothing in Aristotle's argument hinges on it. By 'capacities' Aristotle has in mind whatever it is that is responsible for our being able to experience feelings. The word 'state' translates *hexis*, which literally means 'having' or 'possessing', and is sometimes translated as 'disposition'. Here Aristotle comments that 'by states I mean what we have when we are well or badly off in relation to feelings . . . if, for instance, our feeling is too intense or slack, we are badly off in relation to anger' (1105ba27–9). States of character, then, are certain patterns of feelings and desire and so belong to the non-rational part of the soul (cf. *NE* I.13).

Aristotle presents four arguments for (B) (1105b30–1106a7). Firstly, we are said to be excellent or base because of our possession of virtue or vice, but not because we have certain feelings. Secondly, we are neither praised nor blamed for the feelings we have, but we are praised or blamed for our possession of virtue or vice. Thirdly, we do not decide on the feelings we have, but virtues are decisions or at least imply decision. And fourthly, to experience a feeling is to be moved, but possession of virtue is not to be moved but is to be in some condition. Aristotle thinks the same arguments justify (C), but I will only consider their significance for the truth of (B). But we might think that Aristotle's arguments for (B) are unconvincing.[16] We might, contra argument two, praise a person for merely having a feeling. Imagine a person who is not characteristically compassionate but displays compassion on one occasion: we might praise such a person just because he had that feeling. But this is not quite right: if we praise him, we don't do so *merely* because he feels compassion, but because he feels it on the right occasion and for the right reason. Again, we say, contra argument three, we are moved by a person's generosity and, since generosity is a virtue, we are moved by virtue. But this too is a mistake: Aristotle is not denying that we can have an attitude towards another's character; rather he is claiming that in possessing a virtue one is not moved, whereas in having a feeling one is.

II.6

Although it's true that all virtues are states of character, it's not true that all states of character are virtues. Aristotle discriminates specifically virtuous states of character by claiming that they are 'intermediate' states. This brings us to the 'doctrine of the mean'. The doctrine has been variously described as the 'single most difficult concept in the *Ethics*' (MacIntyre 1967, p. 62); as bold, interesting and 'quite possibly true' (Urmson 1980, p. 157); and as practically futile and of questionable conceptual utility (Barnes 1976, p. 26).

As we have noted before 'every virtue causes its possessor to be in a good state and to perform its function well' (1106a17–18). So, the virtues of a knife, for example, include its being sharp: a knife's sharpness is part of what makes it a good knife and enables it to perform its function well. Whatever the human virtues are, they are what cause us to be good and to carry out *our* function well. We have already been told, in *NE* II.5, that virtues of character are states, which we analysed as patterns of feeling and desire. So, the virtues are going to be those patterns of feeling and desire that make us good and carry out our function well. The patterns of feeling and desire that are virtues are intermediate patterns. This claim merits further consideration.

Aristotle first introduces the concept of the intermediate and distinguishes two senses in which something can be intermediate. He then applies one of these notions to excellence in craft and to virtue of character. Let's consider his initial remarks:

> In everything continuous and divisible we can take more, less and equal and each of them either in the object itself or relative to us; and the equal is some intermediate between excess and deficiency. By the intermediate in the object I mean what is equidistant from each extremity; this is one and the same for all. But relative to us the intermediate is what is neither superfluous nor deficient; this is not one and the same for all. (1106a28–34)

In this passage Aristotle identifies two senses in which something can be intermediate: (a) intermediate in the object and (b) intermediate relative to us. He clarifies the sense of (a) with a numerical example: six is 'equidistant' from both two and ten and so is intermediate (1106a34–b1). He clarifies the sense of (b) with a dietary example: the amount of food appropriate for an athlete will not be the amount appropriate for a child (1106b2–7). There *is* an appropriate amount of food for an athlete and for a child, but the appropriate amount is relative to the particular circumstances. What counts as appropriate will vary from situation to situation, which is not true of the intermediate in the object.

Aristotle thinks that the intermediate relative to us is the differentia of the virtues of character and that this is confirmed by what is excellent in skill because it is often said of something well crafted that 'nothing could be added or subtracted' (1106b12). All that is meant by this, I think, is that something well made could neither be improved by the addition of something nor by the removal of something. The craftsperson gets it 'just right' striking a balance between going 'over the top' and not going nearly far enough. Aristotle applies this notion of the intermediate to states of character in the following passage:

> [Virtue of character] is about feelings and actions and these admit of excess, deficiency and an intermediate condition. We can be afraid, for instance, or be confident, or have appetites, or get

angry or feel pity, and in general feel pleasure or pain both too much and too little and in both ways not well. But having these feelings at the right times, about the right things, towards the right people, for the right end and in the right way is the intermediate . . . and this is proper to virtue. (1106b16–23)

Virtues are intermediate states of character that fall between two opposing extreme states: one of excess and one of deficiency. We have noted above that states of character are patterns of thought, feeling and desire. In order to appreciate fully Aristotle's insight in this passage it is necessary for us to think about the nature of such patterns in a little more detail.

We noted in our discussion of *NE* I.13 that Aristotle thought the non-rational part of the soul was 'obedient to' the rational part of the soul. Consider, for example, an instance in which I leave the house in the morning and see my neighbour slashing my car tyres. I want to hit him. My desire to hit him is part of my feeling of anger towards him; and my feeling of anger towards him is part of my judgement that he has injured me (in damaging my property) without warrant. So my feelings and my desire, which Aristotle locates in the non-rational part of the soul, are obedient to judgement, which Aristotle locates in the rational part of the soul.

Aristotle thinks (surely quite rightly) that there are many different patterns of thought, feeling and desire. For example, a person could place so little value on his property and on himself that he is not angered when he sees his neighbour slashing his car tyres. Since, in this person's estimate, he has not been injured (perhaps he thinks himself unworthy of the slightest respect) he has no desire to hit his neighbour. We may contrast such a person with someone who places so high a value on his property (and on himself) that he is insanely angry when he sees his neighbour slashing his tyres. Since, in this person's estimate, he has been so grievously injured (that car was everything to him) he desires not just to hit his neighbour but to kill him *and* his wife, family and friends in a most sadistic manner.

Aristotle's point is that some of these patterns of thought, feeling and desire are better than others and that the *best* state is the intermediate. The person who has an intermediate state of character correctly estimates the importance of some good as a component of a *eudaimon* life. Such a person will have the 'right feelings at the right time about the right things and towards the right people' because he correctly judges the importance or value of goods in his life. To continue the example above, the virtuous person will be angry with his neighbour because he values his property and the wilful destruction of our property merits an angry response. But he doesn't place such inordinate value on his property, valuing it more than the life of others and more than doing what is right, that he becomes insane and kills his neighbour. This, then, is the sense in which the virtues are intermediate states of character.

Aristotle defines virtue at 1107a1–3: 'Virtue, then, is a state that issues in decisions, consisting in a mean, the mean relative to us, which is defined by reference to reason, that is to say, the reason by reference to which the practically wise person would define it. It is a mean between two vices, one of excess and one of deficiency.' We have already commented on aspects of this definition. It remains for us to examine what Aristotle means when he claims that virtue is 'a state that issues in *decisions*'. The word translated 'decision' here is '*prohairesis*', which Aristotle analyses at length in *NE* III.2–3. We won't consider the concept in detail here, but will note in what way virtuous states of character issue in decisions. It will be recalled from our discussion of *NE* II.1 that although virtues are habituated states they are not themselves habits. Habits can be carried out 'mindlessly' or 'without thought'. A virtuous action, however, is not 'mindless': it is an expression of a person's judgement about the best thing to do in the circumstances (cf. *NE* VI.5). A virtuous person is attentive to his situation and reflects on what he perceives to be its salient features before electing a course of action. So, virtues are intermediate states of character that issue in decisions which are expressed in action.

One source of dissent to the account of the doctrine of the mean we have outlined is that the account is practically useless. The concern is this. Although Aristotle has told us virtues and vices appear in triads (the intermediate flanked by two extreme vices), he has given us no criteria to determine which states are intermediate and which excessive or defective. Without such criteria we won't be able to determine the states we should aim to inculcate in ourselves and in our children: hence the claim that the doctrine is *practically* useless. This objection assumes that it is Aristotle's aim to provide practical advice concerning the acquisition of virtue (cf. 1103b28–30; 1179b2–4). But this assumption is false. In fact Aristotle assumes that his audience will have been well brought up and so may already have the virtues that are under discussion (1095a2–4; 1103b23–24). This criticism, then, is unwarranted.

A more serious objection is that the claim that virtues and vices form triads is false. There are some virtues, for example justice and truthfulness, that do not fit into this pattern. A person may not distribute some divisible good fairly and so be defective and therefore unjust. But in what sense can a person be excessively just? It would be unfair to pretend that Aristotle was unaware of this (1134a1–2) but it nonetheless appears to be a counterexample to the distinguishing characteristic of the virtues in general: hence the claim that the doctrine is 'conceptually empty'. However, even if the claim that virtues and vices are triads is false, this doesn't cast doubt on what I take to be the core of Aristotle's account of the virtues: 'for we are noble in only one way, but bad in all sorts of ways' (1106b35). That is to say, our judgements about the importance of goods in our lives can be mistaken for a variety of reasons. It is characteristic of the virtuous person, however, that his estimate is sound.

II.8

I have skipped over Chapter 7 in which Aristotle nominally fits various virtues and vices into the framework provided by the doctrine of the mean. Since we'll consider some of the particular virtues of character in greater depth later, to review Aristotle's account of them here would result in unnecessary repetition. In *NE* II.8 Aristotle comments on the relationship between the virtues and their opposing vices.

Aristotle has claimed that for each virtue there are two opposing vices. Thus he rejects the view that there is just one vice opposed to the single vice of stinginess. Since generosity and wastefulness appear to be similar, because they both involve giving to others, it may seem that there is no distinction between them.

Aristotle notes that 'sometimes one extreme – rashness or wastefulness, for instance – appears to be somewhat like the intermediate state, bravery or generosity' (1108b32–4). This appearance is responsible for the (erroneous) impression that each virtue is opposed to a single vice. To take up one of the examples Aristotle presents here, on this opposing account generosity is a virtue and is opposed to the vice of stinginess. Generosity and wastefulness have, according to Aristotle, been conflated because of their apparent similarity.

Aristotle rejects this alternative account for two reasons. The first is that one or other extreme just is closer to the intermediate and so we are apt to oppose virtue to the more extreme of the vices (1109a7–9). For example, bravery and rashness both have in common a degree of fearlessness and of standing firm in the face of danger. They differ in that the brave person only stands firm when it is right to do so, whereas the rash person stands firm whether it's appropriate or not. These states, though, are closer to each other than bravery is to cowardice. The coward seldom stands firm in the face of danger and is apt to be afraid of things even when they are not actually frightening. As a consequence of the closeness between bravery and rashness, we might be tempted to think that there is one state (standing firm in the face of danger) which is opposed to cowardice.

The second reason Aristotle presents is that our own perspective colours our appreciation of these matters. If I am a coward, for example, I may perceive both the brave and the rash to be charged with some kind of reckless 'death wish'. To my mind, they both take absurd risks. If, though, I am rash, I may perceive both the brave and cowardly as weak and frightened of everything. So, our own states of character may be responsible for our judging there to be only one vice opposing each virtue.

II.9

In *NE* II.9 Aristotle presents us with some practical advice on achieving intermediate states of character.[17] The first point he makes is that it is hard work to be virtuous (1109a25). It is easy to give or to spend money, but to spend money in the right way, to give it to the right people at the right time, is certainly not easy. As a consequence we regard the achievement of virtue as praiseworthy and fine (1109a30). And I think we can agree with Aristotle on these points, though we may note that the rarity of virtue is not exclusively the source of its value. Since virtue is hard to achieve, Aristotle presents three pieces of practical advice in our efforts to achieve the intermediate.

The first piece of advice is that we should always avoid the extreme more contrary to the intermediate or virtue (1109a30). Aristotle characterizes this as the second-best option after achieving virtue proper itself: 'the lesser of two evils' (a35). The point seems to be that I should tend more towards rashness than cowardice and more towards wastefulness than ungenerosity because rashness is closer to bravery and wastefulness closer to generosity. However, without an independent account of what rashness, bravery and cowardice consist in, this suggestion may be apt to mislead, and precisely because of the point that our 'natural tendencies' differ. For if I am more or less brave, then to be told to tend towards the rash will not help me realize the state of bravery. Of course, this will not be a problem if I know that I am more or less brave, but that is precisely the point. Aristotle has not produced a criterion for bravery and so we have been given no theoretical grounds for determining the nature of the state we possess.

This point further undermines Aristotle's second piece of advice. Aristotle thinks that we should notice our own tendencies and 'drag' ourselves in the opposite direction (1109b3–5). So, if I am aware that I have a propensity for cowardice I should tend towards what strikes me as rashness. But again without some way of determining my 'starting point' such advice is useless.

The final piece of advice Aristotle offers is that we should be wary of pleasure in all things (1109b8–11). Pleasure is responsible for leading us astray and so we should be particularly cautious about those things in which we take pleasure. In conjunction with the advice given above, we may infer that Aristotle thinks we should tend towards the abstemious rather than to indulge our pleasures. In saying this, of course, Aristotle must imagine us to be thinking of the pleasures that are the concern of temperance, for presumably this caution does not apply to the pleasure proper to virtue.

Study questions

1. What are states of character?
2. Why does Aristotle compare virtues to skills or crafts?
3. Does the doctrine of the mean fulfil its purpose?
4. Does Aristotle's list of virtuous states of character exhaust the states we think are admirable?
5. Are there any such things as states of character?

NE III

Introduction

NE III comprises Aristotle's discussion of the nature of responsibility and his discussion of bravery and temperance. His examination of the other virtues of character continues through *NE* IV–V. His discussion of responsibility raises several topics including the nature of voluntary and involuntary action; the nature and role of 'decision'; and the matter of whether we're responsible for the character traits we possess. Although we will focus on the first of these issues, we will briefly comment on the others.

The words 'voluntary' and 'involuntary' translate Greek words '*hekousion*' and '*akousion*'. This translation is, in most contexts, correct, but the general Greek usage connotes, respectively, willingness and unwillingness. In this general sense, to say a person acted *hekon* is to say that he acted willingly. Irwin uses the standard translation and I follow him. As we shall see, our choice of translation has some implications for our interpretation of Aristotle's views about when a person is responsible for his actions.

III.1

Aristotle presents two reasons for his discussion of voluntary and involuntary action. Firstly, virtuous actions are praiseworthy and vicious ones blameworthy. Since only what is done voluntarily is apt to be praised or blamed, Aristotle thinks defining the voluntary and involuntary is necessary for his account of virtue and vice (1109b33–4; cf. *EE* 1223a23). Secondly, Aristotle thinks his discussion will be of use to those in the legal profession who determine the distribution of honours and punishments (1109b34–5).

Aristotle defines voluntary action negatively: every action is voluntary provided it's not involuntary. He then defines an action as involuntary if, and only if, it comes about either 'by force' or 'through ignorance' (1110a1–2). Aristotle thinks each of these conditions is sufficient for an action to be qualified as involuntary. We will examine each of these conditions in turn.

Aristotle claims that an action comes about 'by force' if, and only if, the action 'has an external principle, the sort of principle in which the agent, or [rather] the victim, contributes nothing' (1110a3–4). The point here is that if the cause of the action is external to the agent, the agent acts involuntarily. Aristotle illustrates this with the example of a mariner blown off course by a tempest (1110a4–5). The cause of his going off course was the tempest, which is external to the mariner; hence the mariner is not blamed for going off course.

There are, however, two points to note here. Firstly, it seems that not everything whose principle or cause is internal is voluntary, for example, the beating of the heart and the process of digestion. But Aristotle hasn't said that everything with an internal principle is voluntary, only that nothing is voluntary whose principle is *external*. However, since Aristotle analyses action in terms of the agent's thoughts and appetites (1139a33–5), the mariner, strictly speaking, does not act at all.[18] Aristotle himself appears to signal this by characterizing the agent as a 'victim', which suggests his having been acted upon rather than having acted.

Secondly, Aristotle would not excuse agents whose neglect contributed to the action. For example, if the mariner had been at the bottle and subsequently failed to interpret the meteorological indicators of the looming storm, he'd be blamed for the ship's going off course (Kenny 1979, p. 29). But in that case, of course, the mariner would have contributed to the action by getting himself into a state that impeded his ability to act. With these points noted, the account of acting by force seems relatively straightforward. However, there are more cases in which we want to say a person was 'forced to act' than are captured by Aristotle's definition.

Sometimes we want to say people were forced to act in a certain way because of the threat of something worse (1110a5–6). We may say a person was, for example, 'forced' to hand over his wallet to a mugger wielding a knife and likewise a captain was 'forced' to jettison his cargo to save the life of his crew (1110a10). These cases are much more complicated than those in which the agent contributes nothing (1110a7–8). Aristotle comments:

> These sorts of actions . . . are mixed, but they are more like voluntary actions. For at the time they are done they are choice-worthy, and the goal of an action accords with the specific occasion; hence we should call the action voluntary or involuntary on the occasion he does it. Now in fact he does it willingly . . . hence actions of this sort are voluntary, though presumably the actions without [the appropriate] qualification are involuntary, since no one would choose any such action in its own right. (1110a11–19)

There are two issues that need to be resolved here. Firstly, the precise sense in which such actions are said to be involuntary. Secondly, whether Aristotle thinks agents are responsible for such 'mixed' actions.

I think the sense in which 'mixed' actions are *voluntary* is, on Aristotle's account, reasonably clear. The cause of the person's handing over his wallet is 'internal' in that it can be explained in terms of his thoughts and appetites. However, the sense in which 'mixed' actions are involuntary is far less clear. One suggestion is that Aristotle is, in this passage, using the more general sense of *akousion* that we referred to in our introduction (see, for example, Bostock, pp. 105–6). On this account the person hands over his wallet voluntarily, but *unwillingly* and so his action is 'mixed' in the sense that he both wants to hand over his wallet and does not want to. This reading does justice to Aristotle's claim that in acting by force the agent is pained (1110b13–14).

However, there are two reasons why this interpretation is unconvincing. Firstly, the person hands over his wallet voluntarily and, I think, willingly *given the circumstances*: he *wants* to hand over his wallet to save his life. Secondly, even if the interpretation is right and the person hands it over unwillingly, it just doesn't follow that his action is involuntary. An agent may act unwillingly and nonetheless be responsible for his action. A clear example of this is the *enkrates* or the continent person: he does the right thing reluctantly. However, his reluctance doesn't imply his not being responsible for the action. Indeed the *enkrates* appears to be praised for having done what is 'right' (1145b9–10). So even if Aristotle does mean that in 'mixed' cases the agent acts unwillingly, this does not yet present us with a satisfactory sense in which the action is involuntary.

Aristotle's own comment on the sense in which such actions are involuntary is captured in the cryptic remark that 'no one would choose any such action in its own right' (1110a18–19). One thing he can't mean by this is that the agent didn't choose the circumstances to which he had to respond, because that would render almost *all* actions involuntary for we seldom do choose the circumstances we face in life.[19] How, then, should we interpret this remark? I think Aristotle means that the actions in question are so absurd that, without qualification, a sane person would only perform them by force. No one would simply hand over his property to another person: he would have to be *forced* to do so. This is stronger than, for example, Kenny's claim that a person merely wouldn't *want* to perform the unqualified action (1979, p. 32). Nothing in Kenny's claim substantiates Aristotle's apparent classification of such action as involuntary. For, provided that it does not come about through ignorance, an action is only involuntary if it is forced. Thus it makes sense to connect 'mixed' cases to instances of acting by force.

This brings us to our second question: does Aristotle think agents are responsible for 'mixed' actions? Interestingly, the answer doesn't depend on the sense in which such actions are involuntary because Aristotle gives an independent account of whether the agents of 'mixed' actions are to be praised, blamed or exonerated.

Aristotle rightly notes that determining whether a particular 'mixed' action merits praise or blame is difficult (1110a30). He does, however, make a series of comments that help to clarify his position. People are praised for 'mixed' actions if they are done for 'great and fine results' (1110a20–1) and are blamed if they do what is shameful for 'nothing fine' (1110a23). In other cases, people are not praised but are excused when circumstances are such that they 'overstrain human nature' (1110a26).

Aristotle's first point appears to be that whether we praise or blame an agent for a 'mixed' action depends on the context of the action and, in particular, the agent's reason for acting. If his action was the best response to the situation he may be praised. The captain who jettisons his cargo certainly seems to have performed the best action in the circumstances and might therefore be praised. However, if the agent's action was not the best response he might be blamed. And we certainly have some intuitive sense of this distinction. We don't blame a bank clerk who surrenders money if he's threatened with a gun, but might if he's only threatened with a folk song (cf. *EE* 1225a14–17). Although this is true, it doesn't make clear what constitutes the 'best response' to a given situation. In general, Aristotle seems to think that we are more likely to excuse a person for having done something shameful if it was to avoid something painful rather than to obtain something pleasant (*EE* 1225a24). However, it's clear that praise or blame in such cases does not depend on whether the agent *wanted* to do the action or, without qualification, would have had to be *forced* to do it. It depends on the context of the action and on the agent's reason for acting as he did.

Aristotle also thinks that people should be excused in some cases in which human nature is 'overstrained' (1110a26). Perhaps Aristotle has in mind some very extreme cases, such as certain forms of torture, in which the agent can no longer be accurately said to be acting at all.[20] At the most extreme end of such a continuum we may no longer be able to explain a person's action in terms of his thoughts and appetites, perhaps if he's been injected with some kind of truth serum. Such an action would, on Aristotle's account, be forced. However, there will inevitably be less extreme cases in which we can explain the action in terms of the agent's thoughts and appetites and which we may still want to claim are forced. Praise, blame or exoneration in such cases may depend on what we think people can be reasonably expected to resist (cf. 1150b1–19).

Aristotle concludes his discussion of force by rejecting another sense in which someone might claim to have acted by force. Sometimes people claim they were forced to do something bad because of something pleasant about the action (1110b10). For example, a person may try to excuse his having committed a theft by claiming that he was overcome by the pleasure of possessing the stolen object. Aristotle rejects such excuses on two grounds. Firstly, to accept it would make all actions trivially involuntary because, he claims, an agent always acts because of something pleasant or good (cf. 1094a1–3). Secondly, people perform laudable actions because of something pleasant or good too. Since such actions are apt to be praised or blamed, so too are these actions for which the agent is hoping to be excused.

The second sufficient condition for involuntary action is ignorance. An agent only acts 'involuntarily if he is ignorant of one of these particulars' (1111a3). By 'particulars' Aristotle means any, though not credibly all, of the particular circumstances of the action: 'who is doing it; what he is doing; about what or to what he is doing; sometimes what he is doing it with . . . for what result' (1111a4–6). So I may be said to be acting through ignorance if I believe that I am donating to charity but am in fact the victim of a confidence scam. Presuming that I'd taken reasonable steps to avoid the charge of negligence, I may fairly not be held responsible for my action. Aristotle distinguishes this sense of acting through ignorance from two other senses that he thinks imply culpability.

Firstly, some people claim to have acted in ignorance because they were drunk or angry (1110b26–8). However, what explains the person's action is not his ignorance, but his drunkenness. I don't think Aristotle's view differs very greatly from our own on this point. Secondly, some people claim to have acted in ignorance of the 'universal' (1111a1), by which Aristotle means some kind of general principle. Again Aristotle rejects this explanation: this is precisely the kind of ignorance exhibited by the vicious person who's held responsible for his actions (1110b28–30). Imagine a person claiming that it wasn't his fault that he stole the car because he didn't know stealing was wrong.

Aristotle also introduces a category of action he labels 'non-voluntary'. An agent acts non-voluntarily if he acts while he is ignorant of some relevant particular of his circumstances. However, unlike the person who merely acts through ignorance, the person who acts non-voluntarily feels no remorse for what he's done, even when he subsequently learns of his error. Now, from Aristotle's claim that one is only excused if one acts involuntarily we might infer that he intends to hold the person who acts non-voluntarily responsible. Imagine, for example, that a father gives his son what he thinks is medicine but turns out to be some substance toxic to the child. When he is informed of this, he shrugs because he genuinely doesn't care that he has, albeit unwittingly, caused his son pain. Aristotle claims that the father has acted neither voluntarily nor involuntarily (1110b20–5). What is not clear from the text is whether Aristotle thinks that we should hold such a person responsible for his action. Hughes, for example, thinks that Aristotle is here making a moral rather than a legal point: the father should not be prosecuted but may nonetheless be subject to moral condemnation for his lack of remorse (p. 125). Bostock thinks that the point is irrelevant to the discussion of responsibility because the father acted through ignorance (p. 112).

Urmson, however, presents a subtler and, I think, more accurate account of non-voluntary cases (1988, pp. 45–6). We're not excused for what we've done simply because we're ignorant of at least one of the relevant particulars. Whenever we act we are ignorant of many of the particular circumstances of our action. For example, when I butter my toast I am ignorant of the precise temperature of its crust but it doesn't follow that I butter it involuntarily. So Aristotle cannot mean that ignorance of particulars is sufficient for involuntariness of action. Ignorance of some particular is only relevant if it *would* have made a difference to the person's action. Urmson argues that subsequent regret is indicative that knowledge of the particular would have made a difference and so one may be excused. This seems to me a more convincing interpretation of this curious class of actions.

III.2

In *NE* III.2–3 Aristotle is concerned with the nature of decision (*prohairesis*).[21] His motivation for introducing this notion is controversial. Some commentators argue that in *NE* III.1 Aristotle has only been concerned with necessary, but not sufficient, conditions for responsibility. For children and animals act voluntarily, but are presumably not responsible for their actions (Irwin 1980, p. 125; Kenny 1979, p. 28). Irwin goes on to argue that Aristotle's full account of responsibility must be supplemented by the agent's capacity for decision (ibid., p. 132). Other commentators think that Aristotle's conception of decision is 'over-inflated' and reject it (Bostock, p. 105). However, let's examine Aristotle's stated reason for introducing the notion. He writes: 'Now that we have defined the voluntary and the involuntary, the next task is to discuss decision; for decision seems to be most proper to virtue, and to distinguish characters from one another better than actions do' (1111b5–7).

There are two points to note here. Firstly, virtue has been defined as a state that issues in decisions (1106a4–5): when I act generously it is something I've decided to do and haven't done automatically. Secondly, Aristotle claims that decision is a better guide to character than action. For instance, I may decide to leave work on time to get to my daughter's birthday party but get stuck in traffic. I arrive late to the party but does this indicate that I have a base character? Arguably not, since my decision was to get there on time. The two points are connected, for decision is a better guide to character because, as we shall see, decision implies character, virtuous or otherwise.

The first point Aristotle makes is that all decisions are voluntary but that not all voluntary actions are expressive of decision (1111b8). He dedicates the rest of the chapter to distinguishing decision from a range of other mental phenomena. He compares decision with appetite, spirit, wish and belief and concludes that it is identical to none of them (1111b12). He argues that decision is neither appetite nor spirit because animals have appetite and spirit but do not decide (1111b14). Aristotle argues that decision is not wish because although we can wish for impossible things, we cannot decide to seek them (1111b20–1). People also wish for what they cannot achieve through their own agency, but people can only decide to do what they can achieve themselves (1111b23–5). Finally, Aristotle argues that decision is not belief, though it may imply belief (1111b31–5). Belief he claims is about everything, including what is eternal, but decision is only about what we can do. Furthermore, beliefs can be said to be true or false, whereas decisions are either good or bad (ibid.).

From these brief remarks we can infer some of the characteristics of decision. It is constrained by what it is in our power to do and can be done either well or ill. Aristotle concludes the chapter by stating that 'perhaps what has been decided is what has been previously deliberated' (1112a16–17). And it is the nature of deliberation (*bouleusis*) that Aristotle examines in Chapter 3.

III.3
Aristotle does not begin his discussion by specifying what deliberation is. Instead, he is conspicuously concerned with determining the proper object of deliberation. Aristotle claims that no one deliberates about what is eternal, such as the number of sides of a triangle, nor about matters of fortune because 'none of these . . . is achieved through our agency' (1112a30). Rather, 'we deliberate about what is up to us, that is to say, about the actions we can do' (1112a31–2). So far then the object of deliberation is the actions we are capable of performing. However, Aristotle does not think that we deliberate about everything that is 'up to us'. We do not deliberate about actions in which there is some well-established procedure, whereas we do deliberate about matters 'where the outcome is unclear and the right way to act is undefined' (1112b10–11). So, we might not deliberate about whether to use yeast when baking bread, but might well deliberate about how best to help a friend whose son has been diagnosed with ADHD. Aristotle restricts the scope of deliberation still further and claims that:

> We deliberate not about ends, but about what promotes ends. A doctor, for instance, does not deliberate about whether he will cure, or an orator about whether he will persuade, or a politician about whether he will produce good order, or any other [expert] about the end [his science aims at]. Rather, we lay down the end, and then examine the ways and means to achieve it. (1112b12–17)

It is perhaps tempting to think Aristotle has got the matter wrong here. Whilst it is true to say that we deliberate about the means we need to take towards some end, there appear too to be countless examples of our deliberating about ends. For example, I can deliberate about whether I want to become a doctor or an orator or a politician and, it may be argued, since these are all ends, Aristotle is wrong to claim that only means can be deliberated about. There are two responses here. Firstly, the phrase translated here as 'what promotes ends' is '*ta pros to telos*', which can be understood to cover both those things we consider *instrumental* to the achievement of some distinct end and those things that we consider to be *constituents* of that end (Wiggins 1975–76, p. 224). So I can deliberate about whether to have music at my party, where listening and dancing to the music is part of the goal: *viz* throwing an enjoyable party. The second response is that Aristotle is making a conceptual point here (MacIntyre 1967, p. 68; cf. Cooper 1986, pp. 15–16). Whenever a person deliberates they have some 'fixed' end 'in mind'. So Aristotle can happily concede that we can deliberate about whether or not to be a doctor or an orator. The point is, though, that when we do so it is with a view to some 'fixed' end that we have in mind. In this case the end in question might be the most lucrative or satisfying career.

What, then, is the process of deliberation? It is that process through which we attempt to identify those things that promote 'fixed' ends. Where we discover various things that promote the same end we evaluate them in terms of the *ease* and *fineness* with which they reach the end (1112b16–17). It seems fairly clear that these criteria might, on some occasions at least, conflict: what most easily promotes some end may well not be what most finely promotes it. Aristotle does not comment on the possibility of such conflict, but I think, given his remarks elsewhere, that he would assign priority to fineness because the virtuous person acts for the sake of the fine (e.g. 1115b21). It would seem to be characteristic of him to prefer what promotes an end finely even if it involves his enduring hardship.

Decision, then, is the selection of those things that promote the end that is judged to be right (1113a4–6). To put this in a more modern idiom, we may say that decision is the resolution or intention to act in a certain way. Aristotle calls it a 'deliberative desire', which captures the sense in which it is a desire that is the product of deliberation (1113a12). I will now consider one objection to Aristotle's position that threatens to undermine the plausibility of his account of decision.

Aristotle claims that 'the actions we do on the spur of the moment are said to be voluntary, but not accord with decision' (1111b10). Further, he remarks later that deliberation takes time and that what we call 'quick thinking' is in fact a 'kind of good guessing' (1142b4–7). The worry is this. If each decision must be preceded by an act of evaluative deliberation, then any action not preceded by deliberation will fail to express a decision. However, decision appears to be necessary for virtue, and so all those actions that do not express decisions cannot be said to express virtue. The problem is that we *do* think that acts on the spur of the moment can be said to express virtue (cf. 1117a17–22). Take, for example, the case of the school teacher, Lisa Potts. A man wielding a sword entered her classroom and moved to attack the primary-school children in her class. She immediately put herself between the man and the children successfully protecting them from harm (though she was seriously injured herself). Now, we certainly want to say that her behaviour expressed both virtue and decision, but the line of reasoning we have extracted from Aristotle's text appears to preclude such an interpretation. Lisa Potts didn't have time to deliberate before acting and so her action cannot express a decision. Since her action does not express a decision, it does not express virtue. If Aristotle is indeed claiming this, he is claiming something that conflicts with our intuitions. But it seems to me that it is far from clear that he is making this claim.

We might begin by recalling Aristotle's comment that we deliberate about those matters in which the 'outcome is unclear and the right way to act is undefined' (1112b10–11). This would seem to imply that we do not deliberate about matters in which the outcome is clear and the right way to act is defined. So, Aristotle could say that the right way to act was clear to Lisa Potts and so her action was not preceded by deliberation, and yet still claim that her action expressed a decision. However, to accept this response, in this form anyway, is to deny Aristotle's explicit claim that decision is preceded by deliberation (1112a16). An alternative explanation is to interpret Aristotle as commenting on the structure of decision rather than giving a picture of the psychological process involved. On this account Cooper suggests that deliberation would be exhibited by the agent's ability, after the fact, to explain his action (1975, p. 9). His ability to produce reasons for his actions would indicate the presence of a 'deliberative argument' for the course of action decided upon.

I think Cooper is right that the ability to explain the action demonstrates it to be deliberative in character. But I also think we can identify deliberation in 'quick decisions', but we must reconsider the picture of deliberation and decision that we have ascribed to Aristotle. It seems to me that that process is wrongly construed as necessarily being sustained, focused and heavily reflective. We were hesitant about ascribing deliberation to a person if he didn't seem to have time to think through all the steps and to evaluate them fully in terms of their fineness and ease. However, it doesn't follow that some actions on the spur of the moment betray *no* deliberation whatsoever. We can, I think, identify deliberation and decision in, for example, Lisa Potts' action. She certainly had a 'fixed' end, that of protecting the children in her care, and she certainly selected and adopted one way of achieving that end. She didn't, for example, think the best way of protecting the children consisted in her leaping out of the window and running for safety. It's true that she had to respond quickly and it's certainly true that she didn't have time to deliberate fully on the ease and the fineness of the various ways to achieve the end, but it doesn't follow that her action displayed *no* deliberation. So there would appear to be a continuum in these cases.

III.4

Aristotle has claimed that 'wish is for the end': wish is what fixes the ends, the things that promote what we wish for are the objects of deliberation (1113a15). In *NE* III.4 he considers a puzzle with regard to the nature of wish: do we wish for what is *actually* good or for what is *apparently* good (1113a15–16)? Aristotle first draws out the implications of accepting these interpretations and then attempts to resolve the puzzle.

If, on the one hand, we claim that it is constitutive of wish that it aims at what is actually good, then it follows that no one wishes for what is bad (1113a17–19). For, *ex hypothesi*, for something to be a wish it must be for what is actually good. If, on the other hand, we claim that it is constitutive of wish that it aims at what is apparently good, then it follows that there is no sense in which a wish could be correct or incorrect. For, on this account, all that is necessary for something to be a wish is that it seems to be good to someone: this allows for the possibility of contrary wishes (1113a22).

Aristotle resolves this puzzle by claiming that 'what is wished is the good, without qualification, but for each person what is wished is the apparent good' (a24–5). The point being that we all take ourselves to wishing for what is good but we may go wrong and actually be wishing for what is bad.[22] The virtuous person will wish for the good and will succeed; the vicious person will wish for the good and will fail.

III.5

Aristotle thinks that we are responsible for the character, virtuous or vicious, that we develop (1113b7). The argument that we find for this claim is usually discussed with reference to the problem of free will.[23] I will not directly consider the classification of Aristotle's position with regard to the modern problem, but will note the implications of his argument.

Aristotle's first point is that just as acting virtuously is 'up to us' so is acting viciously (1113b7–8). This is clearly opposed to Socrates' position that 'no wise man believes anyone sins willingly or willingly perpetrates any evil or base act' (*Protagoras* 345e). Aristotle's main argument for the claim that our character is 'up to us' appears to be as follows:

(i)   'A given type of activity is the source of the corresponding state [of character]' (1114a11; cf. 1103b21–2).
(ii) If the actions that resulted in the state of character were 'up to us' then the state too was 'up to us'.
(iii) If something is 'up to us' then we are responsible for it.
∴
(iv) We are responsible for our states of character.

The argument is that states of character are produced by repetition of certain kinds of actions. Provided that those actions were up to the agent, then the agent is responsible for the state he acquires. So, at each point in the past the agent was free not to perform the action that gave rise to his state. Aristotle goes on to claim that 'the person who is [now] unjust or intemperate was originally free not to acquire this character, so that he has it willingly, though once . . . acquired . . . he is no longer not free to have it [now]' (1114a4–5).

Aristotle considers and rejects one objection to premise (ii). The objection states that everyone aims at the apparent good but no one can control how the good appears to him. Therefore, his action is not up to him since it depends on an appearance that is outside his control (1114b1–3). The assumption behind the objection is that virtue or vice is dependent upon the appearance of the good. Aristotle claims that matters are the other way around and that the appearance of the good depends on one's state of character. Let's suppose we pass someone who has fallen in the street. A kind person will notice and will want to relieve any distress. An insensitive person may not notice and will not be motivated to help. The good appears differently to the two characters because of their different states.

One problem with Aristotle's view is his apparent claim that vice is incurable (1114a23; cf. 1121b14). His commitment to this position appears to entail the claim that the vicious agent is not, when he commits his next vicious act, free to do otherwise. However, there are some thinkers who claim that 'could have done otherwise' is a necessary condition of an action's being free and that praise and blame depend on an action's being free.[24]

III.6–9

After his discussion of responsibility, Aristotle begins his account of the particular virtues of character. His approach is fairly uniform: in each case he is concerned to delimit the scope of the virtue and to examine it in terms of the doctrine of the mean. The virtues of character, we have said, are patterns of feeling, thought and desire. A person has a virtue if he correctly judges the value of some good in life and accords it its due place in that life. The reader will also do well to keep in mind the question as to whether the virtues Aristotle examines are the definitive set and, indeed, whether Aristotle imagines them to be.

Aristotle first discusses bravery or courage (*andreia*).[25] Bravery is an intermediate state with regards to fear and confidence (1115a7). Although many things are thought to be fearful, the brave person only feels fear when the occasion merits it. Furthermore, the brave person's estimation of what it is worth exposing oneself to risk for is sound and he stands firm in the face of certain dangers when he judges it right and proper to do so. Aristotle restricts the concern of bravery to those situations in which one is in danger of dying on the battlefield (1115a30–5). This usage is far narrower than ours: we tend to ascribe bravery and courage to people in a wider range of cases. For example, a person may display courage at work when he feels he has to defend a view that is unpopular with his superiors because he thinks it correct. Aristotle allows this, but thinks that such cases are instances of bravery only by resemblance to the central case (1115a15).

One of the first things we notice about bravery is that it doesn't appear to conform to the pattern of the virtues specified in *NE* II.6 (Pears 1980, p. 171). For there Aristotle seemed to claim that one could experience *a* feeling excessively or deficiently (1106b19–20), but here bravery is said to be an intermediate with regard to two feelings, which we can represent below (Urmson 1988, p. 64):

Feeling	Excess	Intermediate	Deficient
Fear	Cowardice	Courage	Nameless
Confidence	Rashness	Courage	Cowardice

It's worth recalling our initial presentation of the part of the soul that 'listens to reason' in *NE* I.13. We commented there that we respond to a situation with feelings based on our assessment of it. These feelings cause certain desires that may be expressed in action. So, Aristotle needn't concede that bravery breaks the mould: confidence is an attitude about one's abilities distinct from, but partly dependent on, one's attitude arising from one's situational assessment. The confident person's estimate of his abilities is such that he thinks he'll be able to do something with success. So, the brave person is one who is scared to the right degree and on the basis of that feeling correctly estimates his ability to confront the present danger.

One worry here is that bravery is not *always* a virtue. Kant comments that bravery can be put to ill-use and so is not always good (Kant 1948, p. 393). In *NE* III.8, Aristotle himself notes five states that resemble bravery, but which do not actually exhibit it at all. For example, some soldiers might charge into a dangerous battle apparently displaying fearlessness, but are actually more afraid of what their superiors might do to them should they not charge (1116a30–2). Other soldiers may appear to be brave by remaining cool when alarms are raised without grounds. Aristotle comments that such soldiers are not brave, they are merely cognizant of the differences between actual and apparent raids (1116b6–8).

Aristotle discriminates bravery on the ground that it is for the sake of the fine (1115b21) and so he would resist Kant's objection on the ground that an action that is not undertaken for the sake of 'the fine' does not express virtue at all. Bravery is not a state of character that enables one merely to control fear, it is that state which enables one to control fear for the sake of the fine.

III.10–12

Aristotle next discusses temperance (*sōphrosunē*). Temperance is an intermediate state with regard to pleasure. From what we know of the virtues in general, temperance must be about taking pleasure in the right way and for the right reason and so on. However, temperance is not concerned with all pleasures and Aristotle's initial discussion clarifies precisely which pleasures are the objects of temperance.

Aristotle claims that temperance is concerned with the place we give to the enjoyment of *bodily pleasures* in our lives. One can't, he thinks, be temperate with regard to intellectual pleasures, such as storytelling (1117b35). Temperance is specifically concerned only with the pleasures of touch and taste (1118a27), which are pleasures of eating, drinking and having sex (1118aa33–4). It may appear that this restriction of the scope of temperance is unwarranted: surely a person may accord too much time in his life to the listening of classical music, for example. But Aristotle makes the restriction because this particular class of pleasures is distinctive: they are those we share with other animals (1118a25–7). Now, it is significant that animals are not rational and, as Aristotle notes at 1117b24–5, temperance is a virtue of the non-rational part of the soul. Again, at 1147b26ff., he refers to these bodily pleasures as 'necessary' as opposed to choice-worthy in their own right. Our desire for the pleasures of touch and taste arise in us independent of the exercise of reason and so we can only 'chasten' our desire for them because they are not reason-responsive as other desires are.

Corresponding to temperance are two vicious states: intemperance and a state sufficiently uncommon for it to be nameless. The intemperate person is excessive with regard to bodily pleasure. This covers, for Aristotle, a range of base tendencies. The intemperate person will derive more pleasure than is right from certain activities (1118b22). He will eat and drink more than is necessary (1118b16–18). Furthermore, he may take pleasure in what is actually hateful and so enjoy pleasures that are wrong (1118b26). Consider, for example, a person for whom the enjoyment of sexual pleasures is so great that he dedicates inordinate effort to the procurement of ever greater and kinky pleasures. In general, the intemperate person places greater significance on bodily pleasure than is justified and he will, as a result, go to greater lengths to procure such pleasures for himself. The deficient state, which Aristotle thinks is nameless, is a sort of 'insensibility' (1119a7). An insensible person derives less pleasure from an activity than is right and, it would seem, seldom takes pleasure in what he does. He fails to recognize the proper place of bodily pleasures in life or, even if he does recognize it, he fails to desire them.

Study questions

1. Does Aristotle successfully provide necessary and sufficient conditions for the voluntariness of action?
2. Why does Aristotle think that a person may sometimes be praised or blamed for a 'mixed action'?
3. Does Aristotle have a coherent account of decision?
4. Is Aristotle correct to argue that people are responsible for the states of character they have?
5. Does Aristotle provide us with convincing reasons for thinking that bravery is limited to action on the battlefield?

NE IV

Introduction

In *NE* IV Aristotle continues his examination of the particular virtues of character. We will not discuss all of the Aristotelian virtues described in this book and will, in fact, only comment on generosity, magnanimity, a nameless virtue concerned with anger, and shame.[26] Aristotle's description of these characteristics is insightful and instructive and is, additionally, of great historical interest regarding those characteristics esteemed in his day.[27]

IV.1

Aristotle begins by discussing generosity (*eleutheriotes*). Generosity is an intermediate state concerned with the giving and, to a lesser extent, the receiving of wealth (1119b26). Aristotle defines 'wealth' as 'anything whose worth is measured by money' (1119b28), which will include property and time as well as money. The generous person has a just and true estimate of the value of wealth and gives in a manner that reflects that estimate.

A generous person aims at the fine in his actions (1120a25), just as is the case in all the virtues of character.[28] Consequently, the generous person gives of his wealth correctly, which means he gives the right amounts to the right people at the right time and for the right reason (1120a26; cf. 1106b21ff.). It follows, then, that a person who gives to others but for some reason other than for the fine is not generous (1120a28).[29] Such a person only appears to be generous but in fact cares more about, for example, currying favour or whatever it is that motivates his giving. It also follows that a person who finds giving of his wealth painful is not generous. Such a person appears to think his wealth could be put to a better use and so only reluctantly gives it to the person who actually merits it.

Aristotle identifies two further characteristics of the generous person. Firstly, the generous person doesn't receive wealth from the wrong source, because although he knows the value of wealth he does not honour it more than he honours the fine (1120a32–3). Secondly, an exhibition of generosity does not depend on the amount that is given but rather on the *state* of the giver (1120b7). A particularly instructive example here is that of the widow's offering at the temple (Luke 21.1–4). Jesus notes that although the rich donated greater sums of money than the poor widow, she gave more than them because while the rich gave what wealth they had to spare, she gave all she had.

Generosity is opposed to the vicious states of prodigality, which represents excess, and ungenerosity, which represents deficiency. A prodigal person gives of his wealth indiscriminately: he may give money to those who do not deserve it and fail to give to those who do; and he may give more money than an occasion merits. This reveals, Aristotle claims, that such a person values the act of giving over the fine (1121b5–6). There are two consequences of this. Firstly, the prodigal person may give even when it's inappropriate to do so because he cherishes giving. Secondly, the prodigal person may well accept wealth from the wrong sources in order to be able to give more. Aristotle notes that such people are prone to indulge flatterers because they are intemperate. In all this the prodigal person does not aim at the fine and this is what explains his vice. Aristotle comments, though, that such a person is at least curable, primarily because of his looming poverty (1121a22). When he has spent all his money he will begin to know its worth.

The ungenerous person, by contrast, is deficient in giving and excessive in taking (1121b19). Aristotle separates these conditions for there are some people, known variously as misers and cheeseparers, who are deficient in giving but who do not go after others' wealth. Such people are content neither to give, nor to take (1121b32). Other ungenerous people, however, are excessive in their taking and are prepared to accept wealth from any source. Aristotle notes some of the degrading trades under whose name this vice is exercised, including usury and pimping. Such people are shameful lovers of gain and prize the possession of wealth over and above that of acting for the sake of the fine.

IV.3

NE IV.3 is concerned with the virtue of magnanimity or 'greatness of soul' (*megalopsuchia*). The magnanimous person thinks himself worthy of great things and is correct in that assessment (1123b2–3). Aristotle thinks that magnanimity is opposed to two vices: vanity, which is the excessive state, and pusillanimity, which is the deficient one. The vain person thinks himself worthy of more than he is and the pusillanimous person thinks himself worthy of less.

I think it fair to say that this virtue has been the object of considerable criticism by modern commentators. Magnanimity has been described as the '*most appalling crown* of the virtuous life' (MacIntyre 1967, p. 76). Ross characterizes the picture Aristotle paints as 'offensive' (p. 215) and Hardie notes the words of an Oxford don who said of the magnanimous man that he is 'a prig with the conceit and bad manners of a prig' (p. 119). And there are certainly some remarks in the *NE* that support these assessments of this virtue.

The magnanimous person is concerned with honour and dishonour since these signify his worth. Aristotle comments that the magnanimous person is moderately pleased when he is honoured by great people (1124a6–7). However, he disdains the esteem he receives from 'just anyone' or for having done something small (1124a10–11). The magnanimous person remembers the good he does, but tends to forget the good done for him and is 'thoughtless' (1124b13–14; cf. *NE* VIII.8). And he tends to surround himself with fine and unproductive possessions since these are a mark of his self-sufficiency (1125a12).[30] This is not the place for a full-scale defence of Aristotle's position, but I will try to suggest that some of this criticism is not well placed.[31]

The first point is that one cannot be magnanimous without possessing the virtues (1124a1–2). That is to say, the magnanimous person is necessarily brave, temperate, generous, and so on. Since one only possesses such virtues if one acts for the sake of the fine, it follows that the magnanimous person acts for the sake of the fine. So, the magnanimous person *doesn't* act for the sake of enjoying a sense of self-importance and this undermines the accusation of priggishness. He acts for the sake of what is fine or absolutely good.

Secondly, Aristotle emphasizes that the magnanimous person is *correct* in his assessment of his worth (1123b1–2). He thinks himself great and he actually *is*. Perhaps philosophers who object to magnanimity as a virtue think that it is offensive to have an estimate of oneself as great, believing that it is proper only for others to make such estimations. However, we regularly require people to make assessments about themselves and esteem them for their ability to do so accurately. Perhaps, then, the worry is that because of his greatness the magnanimous person ends up being a 'trumpet blower', forever going on about how wonderful he is. But Aristotle explicitly denies this too: he is moderate in the company of those people who are inferior to him because it is vulgar to be showy before such people (1124b23–4) and furthermore he doesn't speak about himself because he is not concerned with praise (1125a6–7).[32] However, even though Aristotle can be defended on the particular points here, it is certainly true that less emphasis is laid on this virtue in contemporary society.

IV.5

The virtue concerned with anger is nameless (1125b27). Irwin suggests 'mildness' as a possible label but the difficulty with this is that a person with this virtue will, when the occasion justifies it, be furiously angry, which is just not something the label 'mild' connotes. So although it is cumbersome, I will continue to refer to it as the 'virtue concerned with anger'. This virtue is opposed to the excessive state, which we might call irascibility, and the deficient state, which we might think of as lack of spirit. The virtuous person will be angry for the right reason, towards the right people and at the right time (1125b32–3). He will not remain angry for longer than is appropriate and will readily pardon those who have caused offence (1126a1). An irascible person, however, is moved to anger quickly, towards the wrong people and for the wrong reasons (a14–17). Such a person fails to make a correct estimation about what actually constitutes offence and, as a consequence, is apt to take offence at more actions than actually merit it. He is also likely to be angrier than the offence warrants. Imagine, for example, a person who takes an axe to his neighbours' door because they were up talking with guests until midnight. Aristotle contrasts the irascible person with the bitter person. A bitter person never lets (perceived) slights go: he remembers and is pained by what he takes to be others' wrongdoings against him. Such a person clearly places a value on these apparent slights that is disproportionate to their nature and as a consequence clings to them in a most unbalanced way. A friend told me recently about a school reunion he attended at which a man took his (now elderly) teacher to task in all seriousness about a poor grade on a chemistry report (much to everyone else's embarrassment). He handed this report in when he was 12 (some 38 years earlier) and it contributed in no way to his final qualifications from the school. Such a person may reasonably be thought to have assigned a disproportionate value to this poor grade because in the context of one's whole life such a thing is comparatively unimportant.

Aristotle claims that the deficient state corresponding to the virtue concerned with anger is nameless. However, we might think of such a person as lacking in spirit. People without spirit are apt to let others 'walk all over them' precisely because they do not challenge insults or slights. Aristotle comments that such people appear to be insensible, by which I take him to mean that such people do not even notice that offence has been given. However, we can further imagine such people who cherish a lack of conflict at any cost and would rather accept any consequences than respond to an insult. Such people are spineless.

IV.9

We have skipped over *NE* IV.6–8 in which Aristotle discusses the 'social virtues' of friendliness, truthfulness and wittiness. Instead, let's turn our attention to Aristotle's examination of shame (*aidōs*). Aristotle doesn't think that shame is a virtue because to experience shame is to have done what one judges to be wrong and a virtuous person does what is right. Shame is a feeling (1128b10) and it is of interest to us in terms of our moral development.[33]

Aristotle defines shame as a kind of fear of disrepute (literally, a loss of reputation) (1128b13). What is distinctive about shame is that it requires one to imagine the world as it appears to another and to judge oneself from that perspective. To use Sartre's famous example, a person caught looking through a keyhole will experience shame. This is because he imagines seeing himself at the keyhole from the other's perspective and judges what he sees himself doing. He thereby experiences himself as degraded in the eyes of the other. It is not, of course, necessary that another person is actually present, nor that one believes there to be.

What is of interest here is the difference in the motivation of one who acts or refrains to act out of fear and one who acts or refrains to act out of shame. A person who acts out of fear takes into consideration in his actions his physical, financial and experiential circumstances and acknowledges only those things that threaten them. Take, for example, a person who abides by the speed limit but only because he knows there to be speed cameras in operation. He recognizes that if he were to be caught he would face a penalty and since he knows that the penalty will harm him in some way he acts in accordance with the law (cf. *Republic* 359d–360d). Aristotle thinks people motivated by fear are not virtuous: 'they are worse to the extent that they act because of fear, not because of shame' (1116a31–2). What, then, is distinctive about someone who acts out of shame? A person who acts out of shame appreciates the fine and values the extent to which he acts for the sake of it. Furthermore, a person who refrains from doing what is wrong because of shame necessarily adopts the point of view of the other. Arguably, the ability to adopt a 'common point of view' is a step in one's moral development because it involves the recognition of the other and not just my physical, financial and experiential circumstances.

This brings us to another of Aristotle's points. Shame is only appropriate in the young because it restrains the youth from doing what is wrong. Shame is not an appropriate feeling in more senior people because they ought not to be doing what might be a source of shame in the first place. On this account, then, the capacity to feel shame plays a central role in the development of the moral sense.

Study questions

1. Does Aristotle succeed in accounting for the goodness of generosity?
2. Should we praise the magnanimous person?
3. When is it appropriate to be furiously angry?
4. Why is shame not a virtue?
5. Is the doctrine of the mean successfully applied to the particular virtues of character?

NE V

Introduction

The discussion of the particular virtues of character in *NE* III–IV is followed by extensive treatment of justice (*dikaiosune*) in *NE* V. The structure of this book is, in some respects, obscure, which perhaps suggests that it's a collection of shorter essays on justice brought together later by an editor. But if its structure is obscure, the themes of *NE* V are, at least, quite clear: the distinction between 'particular' and 'universal' justice; the varieties of particular justice; political justice; decency; and the question of whether a person may be unjust to himself. Examination of all these topics is beyond the scope of this commentary and our discussion will be restricted to the first two.

V.1–2

Aristotle dedicates the first two chapters of Book V to the discrimination of two senses of the Greek word '*dikaiosune*' (justice). That the Greek contained this ambiguity seems clear: Socrates exploited it in the *Republic* (331c–332a) when he challenged Polemarchus' definition of justice. Polemarchus analysed justice as giving a person his due and Socrates rejected this, suggesting that a person may have been due the return of his weapon but that this wouldn't be just if he had since gone mad.[34] Aristotle's initial project, then, is to identify the particular virtue of character denoted by 'justice'. He achieves this on the basis that 'if one of a pair of contraries is spoken of in more ways than one, it follows, usually, that the other is too' (1129a25–6). The thought is that if the term 'injustice' has more than one sense, it is likely that its contrary, 'justice', has more than one sense too.

Aristotle states that there are two ways in which the unjust are spoken of: 'both the lawless person and the overreaching and unfair person seem to be unjust. Hence the just will be both what is lawful and what is fair' (1129a33–b1). Aristotle analyses lawfulness as complete virtue towards others. In this sense a person is just if he exercises all the virtues of character not only towards himself and his friends, but also towards those he doesn't know. This is what Aristotle refers to as universal justice. Although some commentators balk at Aristotle's referring to this sense of justice as 'lawfulness', we needn't let the matter detain us. What is at issue is the

distinction between varieties of justice, not Aristotle's alleged assertion that the concept 'lawful' either does, or ought to, imply action
in accordance with complete virtue. Aristotle is quite clear that 'we
are looking for the type of justice . . . that consists in a part of virtue'
(1130a15).

Particular justice, considered as a virtue of character among the
others, is concerned with fairness: it is that state of character that
makes us seek what is fair and avoid what is unfair. Aristotle characterizes particular injustice as motivated by 'overreaching' or
'greed' (*pleonexia*). This is false: being motivated by greed – or
wanting more of some good, or less of some bad, than is right – is
neither a necessary, nor a sufficient condition for acting unjustly.
This is because justice in distribution or rectification, which are the
varieties of justice Aristotle considers in *NE* V.3–4, are determined
without reference to the motive or feelings of the person who effects
the distribution or rectification.

Aristotle tries to support the distinction between justice as fairness and justice as lawfulness by substituting their contraries
and thereby revealing the different senses of justice. For example,
a person who deserts his wife when confronted by a group of
assailants is unjust (unlawful) because he fails to act in accordance
with complete virtue. However, he is not unjust (unfair) because he
does not in this seek to procure more of some good than is right. It's
important to note that Aristotle's strategy need not be affected by his
claim that the motive of unjust acts is greed. The particular virtue of
justice is concerned with the distribution and rectification of
'honours or wealth or anything else that can be divided among the
members of a community' (1130b31). It is clear that the person who
deserts his wife does not thereby effect either a distribution or rectification of such things and is not, on Aristotle's account, unjust
(unfair) irrespective of his motive.

V.3–5

Having taken himself to have established justice as a particular
virtue of character, Aristotle distinguishes the different species of
that virtue: justice in distribution and justice in rectification. As we
noted above, justice in distribution pertains to the distribution of
divisible goods between persons. Consider, for example, two soldiers
on the battlefield who are outnumbered and under siege. One of
the soldiers urges them to flee, but the other notes aspects of their

position to their advantage and reveals how they can successfully defend their post. The soldiers defeat their opponents and, given their bravery, are decorated. It seems natural that the soldier who resisted the call to flee and devised a successful strategy to ensure their victory should receive a higher honour than the soldier who wanted to flee but who stayed to fight. And this is precisely what Aristotle recommends. A just distribution is one in which people receive goods in proportion to their worth. A distribution that apportions more to a person than he deserves is unjust, as is a distribution that apportions less of a good to a person than he deserves. A just distribution requires, then, at least four terms: the parties A and B and the goods C and D. If A is to B as C is to D then the just distribution is A: C and B: D (1131b5–9).

The central issue here is the determination of worth (1131a25–9). Although many people may agree that a just distribution accords with worth, what they think worth consists in may differ. As Aristotle notes, 'supporters of democracy say it is free citizenship, some supporters of oligarchy say it is wealth, others good birth, while supporters of aristocracy say it is virtue'. Aristotle does not provide a ground for selecting a basis for establishing a person's worth and is content to state that the just is 'in some way proportionate' (1131a31).

In *NE* V.4 Aristotle considers justice in rectification, which pertains both to voluntary and involuntary transactions (1131b25). Voluntary transactions include buying, selling, lending, hiring out, and so on; involuntary transactions include theft, adultery, murder by treachery and suchlike (1131a4–9). Given Aristotle's arguments for the claim that a person cannot treat himself unjustly (*NE* V.10) the notion of injustice in *voluntary* transactions may seem self-contradictory. If it's not possible for a person to treat himself unjustly, then how can a person be treated unjustly voluntarily? However, Aristotle has in mind transactions in which the original cause was voluntary. For example, a person agrees to pay a fee to hire out a lawnmower, but upon returning home finds that the lawnmower does not contain a motor. The person voluntarily entered into a contract but only on the understanding that the lawnmower worked. He has, then, been done an injustice by the person providing the lawnmower.

The distinguishing feature of justice in rectification is that is takes no account of the worth of the parties involved. 'Rather, the law looks only at the differences in the harm [inflicted], treats the people involved as equals, if one does injustice while the other suffers it, and one has done the harm, while the other has suffered it' (1132a4–6). The judge in such a case restores to the injured party the loss he has suffered by taking it from the party who has unjustly gained. So, to continue the example above, the person who hired the lawnmower would have returned to him the money he paid to hire it. Aristotle concedes that the terms 'loss' and 'profit' are not always entirely appropriate, particularly in cases of involuntary transactions in which a victim has been injured or murdered. We may add to this that restoration itself in some cases seems difficult: if a person has indeed been murdered the situation cannot be restored. Some commentators, however, liken justice in rectification to British civil law in which a person, if found guilty, may be required to pay restitution to a victim's family (Urmson 1988, pp. 72–3). There may be some truth in this, but Aristotle's principal concern here is the specification of what justice in rectification is, and not in providing an account as to how, in practice, such justice is realized. A similar response applies to the objection that Aristotle's account of justice in rectification fails to act as a deterrent to committing crime (see, for example, Bostock, p. 61). After all, if the worst that can happen to a thief is that he would have to return what he stole, there is little to discourage his recidivism. To sum matters up: restoration of loss is one thing; punishments and deterrents another (cf. 1132b27–31).

Having been told that there are two species of particular justice (1130b30–1131a1), one can be forgiven for being surprised at the introduction of justice in exchange in *NE* V.5. Aristotle notes the Pythagoreans who thought that reciprocity – doing as you are done by – was just without qualification (1132b23), but he explicitly denies that this notion accounts for either justice in distribution or rectification. It does, however, explain justice in exchange in which 'people seek to return evil for evil, since otherwise [their condition] seems to be slavery or good for good, since otherwise there is no exchange' (1133a1–2). The shoemaker, for example, repays the builder who makes for him a house with some proportional good of his own. Money is the common measure that ensures the comparability of goods in exchange. I will not comment on this further but will note that Hardie deemed it a 'pioneering excursion into economic theory' (p. 183; cf. Finley).

Aristotle concludes Chapter 5 with the following remarks about justice and the doctrine of the mean:

> Justice is a mean, not as the other virtues are, but because it is about an intermediate condition, whereas injustice is about extremes. Justice is the virtue in accord with which the just person is said to do what is just in accord with his decision, distributing good things and bad, both between himself and others and between others. (1134a1–4)

It is clear, then, that Aristotle denies, and does not assert, that justice exemplifies the doctrine of the mean, at least not as that notion applies to the other particular virtues of character. It should be recalled that the virtues of character are said to be intermediate states: that is to say, states of character that fall between two opposing extreme states of character. Justice, however, is not an intermediate state in this sense: it does not fall between two opposing extreme states. Rather, the distribution or rectification the just person effects is intermediate between distributing, or restoring, too much or too little. 'He does not award too much of what is choiceworthy to himself and too little to his neighbour . . . but awards what is proportionately equal' (1134b4–6).

We may wonder, though, about the precise significance of the claim that justice is a mean but not in the same way as the other virtues. Some commentators view Aristotle's account of justice as a mean as a 'failure' (see, for example, Urmson 1980, p. 165). Others view this apparent counterexample as having at least 'quite serious' implications for Aristotle's theory of virtue generally (see, for example, Bostock, p. 70). It is perfectly true that if justice is a particular virtue of character and if it fails to exhibit the pattern of virtues of character generally, then we have an instance of the species, virtue, that deviates from the pattern exemplified in the others. It is not true that this amounts to a *refutation* of the account of other virtues of character: everything that has been said about the other virtues of character is consistent with the account Aristotle has given of justice. We are, though, owed an explanation because justice appears to be structurally different from the other virtues of character. For it was claimed in *NE* II.6 that virtue was an intermediate state in which a person has the right feeling or desire for the right reason and in the right circumstances. The particular virtue of justice does not seem to have a specific feeling or desire and in this respect is distinct from the standard account of the virtues in *NE* II. It may be that justice subsumes the other virtues of character, but it remains true that there is not some specific emotion or desire that it correctly regulates.

Study questions

1. Why does Aristotle distinguish particular and universal justice?
2. Why should we consider particular justice a virtue like generosity?
3. Does Aristotle provide a convincing basis for just distributions?
4. Should we consider the failure of the application of the doctrine of the mean to justice to imply the falsity of that doctrine?
5. What's the relationship between friendship and justice?

NE VI

Introduction

The discussion of justice completes Aristotle's examination of the particular virtues of character. In *NE* VI, he considers the virtues of thought, which require discussion for two reasons. Firstly, Aristotle claimed in *NE* II that virtue of character is an intermediate state and that the intermediate is determined by correct reason (1107a1–3). So far the only thing Aristotle has said about correct reason is that it's characteristic of the practically wise person (the *phronimos*) to have and exercise it. He is yet to explain what correct reason is and to state what it says. At the start of *NE* VI Aristotle acknowledges this lacuna and promises such an account. Secondly, complete virtue comprises *both* virtues of character and virtues of thought (1138b35–1139a1). So, the completion of the account of virtue naturally requires examination of the virtues of thought (1139a4).

Although Aristotle examines a range of virtues of thought in *NE* VI, his primary interest lies in practical wisdom (*phronesis*). Practical wisdom is the faculty of the human soul that determines the best action to perform in any particular situation. Sometimes we seem almost to act out of routine and don't appear to reflect consciously on the best action to perform. This can be seen, for example, in the practice of holding doors open for others. Sometimes, however, we are presented with new and challenging circumstances that require reflection. Consider, for example, a friend who confesses to you his having committed a very serious crime and wants to swear you to secrecy. Now, as it happens, Aristotle thinks we exercise practical reasoning in both cases, though it's perhaps less clear in the first.[35] Our aim in examining this part of the *NE* is to understand the nature of practical wisdom, which is analysed in terms of good deliberation that issues in excellent decision.

But if Aristotle's primary interest is the nature of practical wisdom, why does he bother to comment on scientific knowledge (*episteme*) and wisdom (*sophia*) at all? Wouldn't it make more sense for him to dedicate the entire book to a clear exposition of practical wisdom? There are two points to make here. Firstly, Aristotle's account of virtue would be incomplete without examination of the virtues of thought because the virtues of thought are, as we've noted, a part of virtue (1103a15). Secondly, there are similarities between the intellectual faculties of the human soul and so Aristotle recognizes (quite rightly) the need to distinguish practical wisdom from them.

Before we examine the text it's worth noting that, superficially, the organization of *NE* VI is obscure. It doesn't appear to have an obvious structure, the connection between topics – and in some cases, between passages – is not always clear, the exposition is, at times, particularly dense and the description of the characteristics of practical wisdom is scattered throughout the book. For these reasons, it seems worthwhile to have in place a sketch of the entire book, particularly for readers new to the *NE*.

- VI.1: Aristotle begins by noting a division in the part of the soul with reason that corresponds to the division in the non-rational part of the soul (1139a5–7).
- VI.2: He then states that the function (*ergon*) of these parts of the soul is the acquisition of the truth (1139b11) and that the virtues of these parts will be states that determine the truth.
- VI.3–8: Aristotle then distinguishes five virtues of the part of the soul with reason with a view to isolating practical wisdom: scientific knowledge (*episteme*), craft (*techne*), practical wisdom (*phronesis*), intuition (*nous*) and wisdom (*sophia*).
- VI.9: Since practical wisdom implies good deliberation (1140a26–7), Aristotle examines the nature of good deliberation.

- VI.10–12: Other aspects of the intellect relevant to conduct are briefly characterized and the value of the virtues of thought considered.
- VI.13: Aristotle considers the role of practical wisdom in virtue and the Socratic thesis of the unity of the virtues.

VI.1–2

Aristotle thinks there is a division in the rational soul corresponding to the division in the non-rational soul (1139a5–7). One part is concerned with 'beings whose principles do not admit of being otherwise'; the other is concerned with 'beings whose principles do admit of being otherwise' (1139a7–11). Aristotle calls the former the 'scientific' part and the latter the 'rationally calculating' or 'calculative' part (1139a12). To put matters in a more modern idiom, we can say the scientific part is concerned with what is *necessary* and the calculative part with what is *contingent*. Aristotle distinguishes these different parts of the soul on the basis that they are concerned with different things and that these different things are suited to different parts of the soul. We are not given an argument for accepting this principle here and, indeed, it's not obviously true. Let's suppose we grasp the sense of the proposition 'Every body has a shape'. Let's further suppose that we come to recognize that the proposition is true in all possible circumstances. Are we *doing* something different when we recognize that the proposition states a necessary, as opposed to a contingent, truth?

The question above is based on a confusion, which Aristotle's examination of the respective functions of the scientific and the calculative parts of the soul helps to dispel. The function of the rational part of the soul is to grasp the truth, the scientific part aims to establish just what is true (1139a29), whereas the calculative part aims at a 'practical sort of truth' (1139a26). So, the difference between the scientific and the calculative part of the soul is not just that they are, respectively, concerned with necessary and contingent truths. They do different things: the scientific part grasps what is necessarily true about the universe and the calculative part grasps a practical sort of truth. But what precisely is this 'practical sort of truth'? Aristotle claims that it is 'truth agreeing with correct desire' (1139a30). Put like that, the notion of 'practical truth' is far from clear. However, we reasonably interpret Aristotle as identifying practical truth with excellent decision. Although this may seem strange for those of us who think of truth as a property of propositions that accurately state how things are in the world, Broadie suggests that the use of the term 'truth' is appropriate in this context because it implies the *success* of thought (1991, p. 224). So, practical wisdom is that faculty of the soul which judges correctly the best action to perform in a given set of circumstances. It is, then, the successful exercise of thought concerned with action.

Having identified the notion of practical truth, Aristotle then notes that decision, which is the principle, or cause, of action, is the product of desire and goal-directed reason. Since 'thought by itself moves nothing' (1139a35), decision is 'either understanding combined with desire or desire combined with thought' (1139b5–6). It is perhaps tempting to read these remarks in a Humean fashion. Hume, too, thought that action was the combination of reason and desire. However, he was of the view that reason was a mere slave to the passions (*Treatise* II.iii.3). Reason is capable of calculating and establishing facts, but is not by itself capable of motivating action. Although it is tempting to read Aristotle in this way, it is *not* what he means. He thinks desire and other springs of action are susceptible to reason (see, for example, *NE* I.13).[36]

VI.3

We have said that Aristotle is concerned to distinguish practical wisdom from the other virtues of thought. In *NE* VI.3–7 he introduces the virtues of thought and specifies their differentia. He distinguishes scientific knowledge from practical wisdom on two grounds. One concerns its subject matter; the other, the manner of its being taught.

Aristotle states that: 'We all suppose that what is known scientifically does not even admit of being otherwise . . . Hence what is known scientifically is by necessity. Hence it is everlasting [and is] ingenerable and indestructible' (1139b20–4). The subject matter of scientific knowledge, then, is what we would refer to as necessary truths. For Aristotle there are such propositions to be found in mathematics, theology and the natural sciences (*Metaphysics* 1026a18–19). We may note that Irwin's translation of '*episteme*' is perhaps a little misleading here because we do not think that science is concerned with necessary truths. But we need not let this terminological issue detain us. If we accept the principle that a difference in object implies a difference in the part of the soul concerned, and if we accept that the object of *episteme* is necessary truths and the object of practical wisdom is contingent truths, we can see that *episteme* and practical wisdom are not the same (cf. 1140b3). Aristotle's second point is that 'science' can be taught (1139b25). Since he has claimed that *all* the virtues of thought can be taught (1103a16), the contrast with practical wisdom here cannot be that 'science' is teachable but that practical wisdom is not. His point is that what can be known scientifically can be taught through demonstration: either induction or deduction (1139b29–31). This does constitute a contrast because Aristotle says that the truth practical wisdom grasps cannot be demonstrated because 'there is no demonstration of anything whose principles admit of being otherwise' (1140a34–5). This does not imply that practical wisdom cannot be taught in *some* way, just that it cannot be taught in the same way as science. One factor in our development of practical wisdom might be, for example, exposure to stories: perhaps the stories of Solomon. Being shown examples of practical wisdom might amount to something like teaching, even if it is not teaching through demonstration. So, practical wisdom is not science because it is not concerned with truths about what is necessary and because it can't be taught by means of demonstrative proof.

VI.4

Since practical wisdom is concerned with what can be otherwise, it belongs to the calculative part of the soul (1139a5–15). There is, however, at least one other virtue of the calculative part of the soul: craft or skill (*techne*). In *NE* VI.4 Aristotle distinguishes craft from practical wisdom. This may not, however, be obvious from the text because there Aristotle explicitly contrasts action (*praxis*) and production (*poiesis*) rather than practical wisdom and craft (1140a1–2). However, practical wisdom is concerned with action and craft with production, so Aristotle is effectively asserting a distinction between them.

It is worth recalling that Aristotle is impressed by similarities between craft and virtue: both involve our knowing what we're doing (1105a32–b3) and both are acquired in a similar manner (1103a32–b2). Furthermore, skilled people are able to do what is best in some particular situation. A (good) plumber, for example, is able to diagnose correctly and fix a problem with a drain. So it might seem that practical wisdom is just another skill that happens to be concerned with action. Nonetheless, Aristotle claims that the 'state involving reason concerned with action is different from the state involving reason concerned with production' (1140a3–4). This can be seen by examining his definition of a craft: some state *S* is a craft if and only if *S* is a state involving true reason that is concerned with production, in which the principle is 'in' the producer and not the product (1140a6–15).

This definition does not immediately appear to distinguish craft from practical wisdom because the best thing to do on a given occasion might (aim to) produce something. Imagine, for example, that a friend is upset and you decide that the best thing to do is to comfort him. Is it not the case that you aim to produce a comforted state in your friend? But this is to misunderstand the sense in which Aristotle is using the term 'action'. In this context he uses the term to refer to those things done for their own sake or for the sake of the fine (1139b3–4; 1140b7–8). If the goal of your activity is something other than that activity itself – if, for example, your aim is to comfort your friend so you can borrow his car – then you are not, strictly speaking, *acting* at all. You are trying to win a favour. On the other hand, if your goal is simply to perform the best action in the circumstances – your aim is to comfort your friend because that's the best thing to do – then you are, strictly speaking, *acting*. The contrast between craft and practical wisdom, then, is the contrast between those things done for the sake of something other than themselves and those things done for their own sake. Interpreted in this way, Aristotle is not, absurdly, claiming that things can be produced without activity; he's just claiming that the activity involved in production aims not at acting well itself, but at making the product.[37]

Aristotle makes two additional points of contrast in *NE* VI.5. He writes: 'There is virtue [or vice in the use] of craft, but not [in the use of practical wisdom]. Further, in craft someone who makes errors voluntarily is more choice-worthy; but with practical wisdom, as with the virtues, the reverse is true' (1140b23–5).

The first point here is that we wouldn't deny that someone had a particular skill just because he used it despicably. One vivid example is that of the character Christian Szell in the film *Marathon Man*. Szell is a dentist, and a Nazi, who uses his skills as a rather chilling means of extracting information from a helpless and cavity-stricken Dustin Hoffman. We would, however, deny someone was practically wise if he used his intellect to achieve something despicable. Imagine a person who uses his knowledge of human feelings and aspirations to dupe a person into giving him money. Aristotle's point, then, is that craft does not imply that the end one is aiming for is fine; whereas practical wisdom does imply that one aims at the fine because it *is* a virtue.

The second point, here, is that those who voluntarily make mistakes in craft are superior to those who make them involuntarily (1140b23–4; cf. *HMi* 375c). Although both people make a mistake, the person who does so intentionally is more skilled than the person who does so unintentionally because he could, should he have so chosen, have avoided it. Aristotle claims that with virtue and practical wisdom, the 'reverse is true' (1140b25). A person who voluntarily does what conflicts with what practical wisdom prescribes is worse than one who does so involuntarily. For the person who does so involuntarily might not have acted contrary to practical wisdom (cf. *NE* III.1 *passim*).

VI.5

Let's summarize the results of Aristotle's discussion to this point. Practical wisdom is an intellectual faculty that is distinct both from scientific knowledge and craft. Scientific knowledge is concerned with what is necessarily true, whereas both practical wisdom and craft are concerned with what is contingent. Practical wisdom and craft differ in that the end of practical wisdom is action whereas the end of craft is a product.

In *NE* VI.5 Aristotle begins his positive account of the nature of practical wisdom, though he continues to make further qualifications and additions throughout the book. His first suggestion is that we can clarify the nature of practical wisdom (*phronesis*) by examining the function (*ergon*) of the person who possesses and exercises it (the *phronimos*) (1140a25; 1141b11–12). He comments that: 'It seems proper to the [person of practical wisdom] to be able to deliberate finely about things that are good and beneficial for himself – not about some restricted area – about what sorts of things promote health or strength, for instance – but about what sorts of things promote living well in general' (1140a26–8). Since practical wisdom is concerned with action (1140b5) and the principle of action is decision (1139a34), we can infer that it is characteristic of the person of practical wisdom to make decisions. Aristotle also claims that practical wisdom is a virtue (1140b25), which implies that the practically wise person makes excellent decisions (1144a20). But what are these decisions about and on what basis does the person of practical wisdom make them? Aristotle tells us that the practically wise person is concerned with what is good, or best, for human beings in general.

We might be a little concerned by the claim that a practically wise person deliberates about what is 'good and beneficial *for himself*'. This could be interpreted as an expression of Aristotle's alleged ethical egoism: the curious view that people are obliged to pursue what is (narrowly) in their self-interest. But Aristotle is, in fact, quite careful to avoid such an interpretation. In *NE* VI.8 he notes that the kind of blinkered self-concern implied by the doctrine of ethical egoism '[often] monopolises the name "practical wisdom" that [properly] applies [to all types] in common' (1141b31–2). Furthermore, Aristotle distinguishes self-love, which he thinks is proper, from selfishness, which he thinks improper (*NE* IX.8 *passim*). What is, of course, true is that the practically wise person makes decisions about what he *himself* can do in the circumstances (1112a31–2).

So, the person of practical wisdom characteristically makes excellent decisions about the best actions to perform in any set of circumstances. He arrives at these decisions through deliberation. Now, we have already examined the nature of deliberation in *NE* III and Aristotle considers the nature of good deliberation in *NE* VI.9 so I will reserve detailed comments on it until then. For now, though, it will be useful to have a rough idea of what Aristotle is referring to. Deliberation is that process of considering and estimating the relative importance of aspects of the situation in which the person of practical wisdom finds himself. The outcome of this deliberation is the determination of the best thing to do in light of that assessment. Consider the following example.

One of your colleagues, Jeff, has very poor personal hygiene. It is so bad that he has become an object of ridicule in the office. Since his job involves his meeting clients, your employer is aware that Jeff is, on occasions, the 'face of the company'. What should he do? Well, consider these possible responses: (a) your boss walks into the office one day, screws up his face, points at your colleague and announces, 'Jeff, you stink'; and (b) your boss realizes that the matter is a sensitive one and decides to put on a 'well-being' programme citing a reference from a recent newspaper article in which it is noted that people working in the City don't have enough time to take care of themselves. In response (a) your boss displays absolutely no sensitivity whatsoever: he has failed to judge the impact of drawing attention to Jeff's problem in the presence of his colleagues and has publicly embarrassed him. In response (b) your boss has recognized that there is a problem and has decided on a course of action which reflects his having thought about the difficulties of dealing with these sensitive matters. Response (b) involves the exercise of practical wisdom: the deliberation of the best way to act given an understanding of a situation.

We are now in a position to make some sense of Aristotle's explicit definition of practical wisdom at 1140b5–7: 'Practical wisdom is a state grasping the truth, involving reason, concerned with action about things that are good or bad for human beings.' There is a clear reference here to the notion of practical truth developed in NE VI.2. Aristotle analysed the notion in terms of the combination of correct reason and desire (1139a24–6). This implies, as we have noted above, that a person is not practically wise if his desire does not 'agree' with his reason (1140b22). To be practically wise one must make an excellent decision, which comprises a correct judgement about the best thing to do and an active desire to realize it.

VI.6

This short section introduces the virtue of *nous*. This is variously translated as 'intuition', 'intellect', 'understanding' and 'comprehension'. However, given its rather precise function, I will not translate the term and trust that the reader will appreciate its sense from a specification of that function.

Aristotle has claimed that scientific knowledge grasps necessary truths about the world that are demonstrated from first principles (1139b25–31). What exactly does Aristotle have in mind here? Well, for our purposes, we may consider first principles the most basic truths of a field of study. Take, for example, the Euclidean axioms, such as 'a line is the shortest distance between two points'. From axioms such as these follow the truths of geometry. However, we must have some way of grasping the truth of these axioms given that no demonstration of their truth is possible. If their truth could be demonstrated, it would imply the existence of even more basic axioms on the basis of which such a demonstration could take place. Aristotle claims that *nous* grasps these principles (1141a9).

As we shall see in *NE* VI.7, *nous* completes the state of wisdom (*sophia*), but it is referred to again in *NE* VI.11. There Aristotle announces a faculty analogous to *nous* that is exercised in practical wisdom. We shall consider this faculty in more detail in our examination of that chapter.

VI.7

Aristotle begins by analysing wisdom (*sophia*) as '*nous* plus scientific knowledge' (1141a18), which he characterizes as grasping the truth of first principles and making correct inferences from them (1141a16–17). He then asserts that wisdom is the 'most excellent science' (1141a19) and evidently thinks that it is the finest state a human being can possess and exercise (cf. *NE* X.7). He gives two reasons for this judgement.

Firstly, Aristotle assumes that the value of these respective states is determined by the value of their objects. Since human beings are of inferior value to the other beings composing the universe, it follows that the state concerned with the good of human beings is inferior to the state concerned with the nature of the universe (1141a20–2). Aristotle's assumption seems to some extent to be supported by our intuitions. It's true that we do assign different values to things but we might question the truth of the assertion that the other beings composing the universe are of superior importance to human beings. One natural thought is that the phenomenon of the universe is in all its manifestations equally astonishing and bizarre: from the genesis of stars to the very existence of life at all.

Secondly, 'the content of wisdom', Aristotle claims, 'is the same in every case, but the content of practical wisdom is not' (1141a25–6). His point is this: wisdom is concerned with necessary truths, propositions that cannot be false. Practical wisdom, however, is concerned with contingent truths relative to a particular individual's circumstance. There lurks in the background here the Platonic thought that what is permanent and unchanging is superior to what is perishable and mutable. And perhaps this explains why Aristotle assigns a superior value to the beings that compose the universe.

Having compared the respective values of the states of wisdom and practical wisdom, Aristotle makes some remarks about the nature of practical wisdom. The first – that the 'unqualifiedly good deliberator is the one whose aim accords with . . . the best good . . . achievable in action' (1141b14) – anticipates the examination of good deliberation in *NE* VI.9, to which we shall turn in a moment. The second is contained in the following passage:

> Nor is practical wisdom about universals only. It must also acquire knowledge of particulars, since it is concerned with action and action is about particulars. That is why in other areas also some people who lack knowledge but have experience are better in action than others who have knowledge. For someone who knows that light meats are digestible and [hence] healthy, but not which sorts of meat are light, will not produce health; the one who knows that bird meats are light and healthy will be better at producing health. And since practical wisdom is concerned with action it must possess both [the universal and the particular]. (1141b15–23)

This is the first reference in *NE* VI to 'universals' and 'particulars'. It is by no means immediately clear what Aristotle means by them, nor indeed why reference to them is necessary at this point in the discussion. Let's start by considering what 'universal' and 'particular' mean in this context, bearing in mind that Aristotle makes further reference to them at 1142a25–31 and 1143a27–b10.

The reference to 'universals' is to general truths about what is good for human beings. To exercise practical wisdom a person must have some idea – however bald – of what is good and bad for human beings (cf. *NE* VI.5). In this passage Aristotle states that this is not sufficient: a person merely in the possession of such general truths about human beings will not succeed in acting well.[38] Actions, we are told, are about 'particulars' and so, without some grasp of 'particulars', a person cannot exercise practical wisdom. The truth of this claim depends on what 'particulars' are supposed to be. Aristotle uses the term 'particular' (*kath'kekaston*) in several ways: to refer to particular instances, particular objects, particular types and particular situations. The example in the cited passage suggests that Aristotle has in mind particular *types* in that if I do not know what *types* of meat are light I will not be able to procure and ingest them. But in general the particulars Aristotle seems to have in mind are particular instances: concrete examples of actions we have witnessed and learnt from. In learning from these particular instances we develop a 'sense' of the right way to respond even if we would be hard-pressed to articulate this linguistically. Some people, through exposure to particular instances, may have a very good sense of the right way to respond even if they have not articulated general truths about what's best for human beings.

Turning to the second matter, we might wonder why Aristotle introduces this characteristic of practical wisdom at this point. It should be remembered that Aristotle identifies this characteristic while comparing and contrasting practical wisdom with wisdom. Wisdom is concerned with 'universals' or necessary truths and so it is a legitimate point of contrast that practical wisdom, whilst sharing in what universals there are in its domain, is distinctive in its concern for particulars too.

VI.9

As I noted above, in this chapter Aristotle analyses the notion of 'good deliberation'. This is necessary to clarify further his analysis of practical wisdom, which is analysed in terms of good deliberation. In a series of short arguments, Aristotle rejects analyses of good deliberation as (i) scientific knowledge (1142b1–3), (ii) 'good guessing' (1142b3–7) or (iii) belief (1142b7–9). I will not examine these arguments: they present no special problems. Instead, let's consider the positive account Aristotle gives of good deliberation.

As we noted above, deliberation is the consideration of the relative importance or value of aspects of situations in which we find ourselves with a view to identifying the best thing to do in those circumstances. As Aristotle notes here, this process is not in itself distinctive to the practically wise person (1142b18–19). A vicious person will assess the relative importance of various aspects of his situation and of the various alternative actions available to him, but he will go wrong in his estimation of their *actual* importance. Consider, for example, an irascible person. Let's suppose that this person is queuing for a train ticket and that the woman ahead of him is going through the process of purchasing an annual railcard, which includes the completion of several forms. The irascible person's train pulls into the platform, but the woman has not completed the process of purchasing her railcard. At this, the irascible person berates the woman, telling her she should be more considerate to others and that thanks to her he'll miss his train to his 'very important meeting'. We can see in this a process of deliberation. The irascible person has attended to what, in his estimation, are the significant aspects of the situation: his need to catch a train, the importance of his meeting and the importance of the woman's purchasing her railcard. He has furthermore made a judgement about the situation: the woman has intentionally, and without warrant, injured him. This has led him to select an 'appropriate' response to intentional injury: a loud and violent rebuke.

What is distinctive to the practically wise person is *good* deliberation (1141b11; 1142b33). Good deliberation is characterized by its 'reaching' or attaining some good (1142b22). That is to say, the person who deliberates well identifies what is *actually*, all things considered, the best thing to do in the situation. The irascible person does not correctly identify what is best because, although on some occasions a rebuke is the best action to perform, it only *appeared* to be so in this context because of his vicious state of character. However, it is not sufficient that one arrives at a correct judgement about the best action to perform. For a person to deliberate well it is necessary that he arrive at this judgement through true inference (1142b23–6). Aristotle's point is that we wouldn't count as practically wise a person who only performed what was, as a matter of fact, best but only because of some mistaken belief of his.

The last point we need to consider here is contained in the following, controversial passage:

> Deliberation may be either good without qualification or good only to the extent that it promotes some [limited] end. Hence unqualifiedly good deliberation is the sort that correctly promotes the unqualified end [i.e. the highest good, *eudaimonia*], while the [limited] sort is the sort that correctly promotes some [limited] end. (1142b29–34)

The *eudaimon* person deliberates well with regard to what is unqualifiedly good. The truth of this can be seen through considering deliberation with regard to some 'limited end'. Imagine that we are trying to select the tool to sand a door that has warped and catches on its frame. If we are to be successful in this task, we must have some conception of the 'best tool for the job'. We might want something that will remove the troublesome, swollen wood quickly and effectively, but additionally something that will not be so aggressive as to damage the rest of the door. With that in mind, we can then appraise the various tools before us and make some judgement about which one best fulfils the criteria. If we had no conception of the best tool in mind, on what basis could we possibly make a *good and reasoned decision*? Aristotle thinks the same is true for the kind of deliberation characteristic of the practically wise person. If he has no conception of *eudaimonia*, he will not be able to make good and reasoned decisions about how to act in the best way.

This claim is controversial for several reasons, most of which go beyond the scope of this text. However, we will consider below the most salient. Firstly, do we have such a conception? Secondly, how do we acquire that conception? And thirdly, what is the content of that conception?

With respect to the first question, I take it to be true that we do have some conception of the sort of life we want to live when we make decisions. However, for a person to have a conception of the supreme good, it is necessary that they have thought about and reflected on the value and importance of goals. Broadie claims that we do not have a 'fully worked out conception of the best life' (1991, pp. 198ff.). This may well be true: as we noticed in Section II, a person may give precedence to certain goods in his life unthinkingly and so not thereby have a conception of the supreme good. However, it nonetheless seems possible for a person to reflect on the ultimate goal in life and thereby develop *some* conception of the best life even if that conception is not 'fully worked out'.

With respect to the second question, our conception of the best life evolves through our lives. A person may in late adolescence think the acclaim of others is the maximally important component of a good life and thereby arrange his activities to try to procure such acclaim. But experience may reveal to him that to be celebrated in such a way is not the 'be all and end all' of a good life – as indeed celebrities themselves often remark in interviews. Our conception of the best life is itself, then, the object of deliberation, a point Irwin's translation captures nicely with the phrase that good deliberation 'correctly *promotes* the unqualified end'. As we saw in our examination of *NE* III, the phrase '*pros to telos*' is generally agreed to connote what is instrumental and what is intrinsic to the end. There seems, though, to be a problem hereabouts. Aristotle has claimed that deliberation must be with regard to some end. If we are to deliberate about our conception of *eudaimonia* then this too must be done with reference to some end. The problem is that since *eudaimonia* is the ultimate end, there doesn't appear to be such a further end to which we may refer. This problem is connected to the third question about the substantive content of our conception of *eudaimonia*. Aristotle doesn't spell out the content of his conception of a *eudaimon* life in *NE* VI. Some commentators think the account supplied in X.6–7 plays this role: there Aristotle claims that the activity of contemplating necessary truths about the nature of the world is the best activity we can engage in. However, I won't consider this suggestion further and will just make a couple of closing remarks.

Firstly, let us note that the problem is a very real one: although some people are very confident about what a good human life is like, many are increasingly apt to reserve judgement about the correctness or otherwise of some such conception. Indeed we are today rather uneasy about passing such judgements at all – except perhaps about lives lived at the extremes. Secondly, the problem is seemingly responsible for the sense of 'being lost' that we sometimes feel. If only, we imagine, we knew what we were *supposed* to be doing – what a good human life involves – living itself would be so much easier. One thought, though, is that the deliberation we subject our conception to, to the extent that we do, is in light of our lived experience (cf. 1143b6–14). The adolescent 'tried out', as it were, the idea that a good life was all about the acclaim of others. Through having that as his goal he was able to see whether it seemed to be the most satisfying and worthwhile way to live. Perhaps his recognition of his enslavement to the judgement of others, characteristic of such a life, revealed to him that he did not fully express other aspects of living, such as his autonomy, when subject to such conditions. This remains, though, both a serious problem in the *NE* and in each of our lives.

VI.11[39]

As we noted in our discussion of *NE* VI.7, in this chapter Aristotle makes some further remarks about the role of *nous*, or perhaps of something analogous to it, in the exercise of practical wisdom. *Nous*, you will recall, was initially introduced as that virtue by means of which we grasp the first principles of scientific knowledge. The relevant passage in *NE* VI.11 is at 1143a36–b6:

> *Nous* is also concerned with the last things, and in both directions. For there is *nous*, not a rational account, both about the first and about the last. In demonstrations *nous* is about the unchanging terms that are first. In [premises] about action *nous* is about the

last term, the one that admits of being otherwise . . . for these last terms are beginnings of the [end] to be aimed at, since universals are reached from particulars.

The passage is controversial and[40] a full discussion of it is not possible here – the reader should follow the references provided in the notes. However, we can, I think, make a few remarks to elucidate Aristotle's rather cryptic comments.

Aristotle claims that the practically wise person exercises *nous* in his grasping how matters are in a particular situation. That the person of practical wisdom must grasp the particular situation he's in is something we have already acknowledged above. Here Aristotle claims that *nous* is responsible for that grasp: the practically wise person sees that the situation is thus and that some particular action is best. The point made here recalls our earlier discussion in which we noted that the practically wise person develops a sense for the right way to respond and that it is through the activity of *nous* that he grasps this. This is because Aristotle thinks that the decisions arrived at through practical deliberation cannot be demonstrated (1140a33–5).

VI.12

The first thing to note here is Aristotle's consideration of the value of the virtues of thought. Comment on this issue is merited because there appears to be a 'puzzle' about the use of these virtues (1143b19). Wisdom is concerned with necessary truths about the universe and so appears to have very little to do with human *eudaimonia*. Practical wisdom, on the other hand, is about human *eudaimonia* but nonetheless seems useless to both the good and the aspiring good. Useless to the good because in virtue of being good they will do what is right; useless to those aspiring to goodness because they can easily consult a person who possesses practical wisdom, just as we consult doctors about ailments without trying to acquire full medical knowledge ourselves (1143b28–33). Aristotle rejects these ideas. Firstly, he opposes the idea that a state of the soul is valuable only if it is productive (1144a1–2). Secondly, he claims in any case that the virtues of the soul *are* productive in the sense that the possession and exercise of them are partly constitutive of *eudaimonia* (1144a4–20).

The second thing to note is the role of practical wisdom in virtue. Aristotle famously claims that the virtues of character imply practical wisdom and practical wisdom implies possession of the virtues of character. His thought seems to be this. The virtues of character are, as we have said, states that produce patterns of emotional and desirous responses as a result of a person's recognizing something as being of value to him. These states make the virtuous person sensitive to those aspects of situations that are relevant to our deciding what to do. A brave person is sensitive to danger and to the value of his life. A generous person is sensitive to the value of property and time and so on. The virtues then alert us to the relevant particulars of a situation – that we grasp by *nous* – and, if necessary, deliberate about in light of our conception of the best life, *eudaimonia*. This intimate relation between the virtues of character and practical wisdom is further developed in Aristotle's comments in the next chapter.

VI.13

Aristotle begins *NE* VI.13 by introducing the notion of 'natural virtue' (1144b4–7): 'each of us seems to possess our type of character to some extent by nature; for in fact we are just, brave, prone to temperance . . . from birth'. This initially seems to conflict with Aristotle's statement at 1103a25 that we don't acquire virtues of character by nature. It becomes clear, though, that what are in view here are states from which the rational part, practical wisdom, is absent. This is something certainly supported by experience: during their early years children display distinctive temperaments. One child may seem prone to sharing, another entirely reluctant to. But it is important not to confuse this with virtue properly so-called. For Aristotle notes that without the governance provided by practical wisdom these natural virtues can be damaging to their possessor. For example, a child who is naturally prone to sharing may offer what she has to others, who take advantage of her, taking more than they should and so on. The child has exercised her state without that sensitivity to the situation which is characteristic of virtue properly so-called. Aristotle concludes this discussion by claiming that full virtue, comprising both virtue of character and virtue of thought, requires practical wisdom (1144b17).

Aristotle concludes *NE* VI with a qualified endorsement of the thesis of the unity of virtues that he attributes to Socrates. The thesis of the unity of the virtues is the claim that there is really just one virtue, practical wisdom, of which the various virtues, for example, bravery and generosity, are instances. Aristotle rejects this claim. However, he asserts that 'we cannot be fully good without practical wisdom [nor can we be] practically wise without virtue of character' (1144b31–2). This view may strike us today as false. Surely a person can be, for example, generous and yet fail to be brave. Aristotle claims that this is true of natural virtues (i.e. those virtues not governed by practical wisdom) but false of virtues properly so-called (1144b35–7). His thought seems to be this: a person who correctly judges, all things considered, the best action to perform must be sensitive to all the relevant features of the circumstances he is in. To be sensitive to all the relevant features of the circumstances he is in, the person must have the virtues of character (which disclose to him what is relevant about those circumstances). So, a person cannot exercise practical wisdom without exercising the virtues of character. It may well be wondered, however, whether the list of virtues at *NE* II.7 is sufficiently comprehensive to fulfil this task.

Study questions

1. What is the practical kind of truth grasped by practical wisdom?
2. What distinguishes practical wisdom from the other virtues of thought?
3. Why does Aristotle think practical wisdom is a virtue?
4. What is the significance of Aristotle's not providing a detailed characterization of the *eudaimon* life?
5. What is the value of the virtues of thought?

NE VII

Introduction

NE VI brings to a close Aristotle's examination of virtue. In *NE* VII he turns his attention to the phenomenon of *akrasia* and pleasure. There are two discussions of pleasure in the *NE*: VII.11–14 and X.1–5, neither of which makes reference to the other and each of which appears to give different accounts of what pleasure is: in *NE* VII pleasure is analysed as unimpeded activity of the natural state of the soul; and in *NE* X pleasure is analysed as an end that completes an activity. In this commentary I take Aristotle's intention to be captured in his remark at 1152b25–6 that he is trying to show the falsity of arguments for the claim that pleasure is not the, or even a, good.

Aristotle thinks there are three conditions of character to be avoided: vice, *akrasia* and bestiality (1145a16). The nature of vice has already been considered in Books II–VI and we'll say nothing more about it here. Nor will we comment on bestiality, that rare condition of character from which the rational element is entirely absent: a condition 'less grave than vice, but more frightening' (1150a1). Our focus here is on the curious phenomenon of *akrasia*: that condition of character manifested in people who typically judge, all things considered, the best thing to do in a given set of circumstances, but who nonetheless fail to do it.

Socrates, recall, is represented as denying the existence of any such condition, arguing that apparent instances are to be explained in terms of ignorance (*Protagoras* 352B–358E). Aristotle rightly notes that Socrates' denial conflicts with the intuition that *akrasia* exists (1145b28); an intuition strengthened, perhaps, by our personal experiences. But we must be careful not to exaggerate the significance of these experiences. Firstly, Aristotle conceives of *akrasia* as a condition of character: he has in mind a person who *habitually* does something other than what he judges the best thing to do, as opposed to someone who experiences occasional lapses. Secondly, when examining examples we must be sure that what we have before us is an instance of *akrasia* as characterized above and not another phenomenon that might, with fairness, be described as 'weakness of will'.[41]

Aristotle's explicit intention is to identify the sense in which a person who does something wrong because of his sensual appetites or his spirited feelings can be said to know, or believe, that he should have done something else (1146b9–10). Aristotle thinks there is *akrasia* about bodily pleasures and *akrasia* about spirit. We should note that this restriction is not shared by some contemporary thinkers who are generally concerned with how a person can act contrary to his better judgement because of any feeling, not just the pleasures that are the concern of temperance, nor the feelings of spirit. We'll consider Aristotle's reasons for this restriction below.

A note about translation: the term '*akrasia*' is variously translated as 'weakness of will', 'incontinence' and 'lack of self-control'; and the term '*enkrateia*' correspondingly as 'strength of will', 'continence' and 'self-control'. A person who exhibits *akrasia* is referred to as an *akrates;* and a person who exhibits *enkrateia* is referred to as an *enkrates.* The selection of an appropriate translation is difficult because the different translations emphasize different aspects of the conditions. Matters are further complicated by Aristotle's identification of two varieties of *akrasia*: weakness and impetuosity (1150b20). Here, as elsewhere, I will sidestep the issue by using the Greek terms.

VII.1–2

In *NE* VII.1 Aristotle sets out the appearances regarding *enkrateia* and *akrasia*. He notes, for example, that *enkrateia* is considered a praiseworthy condition and *akrasia* a blameworthy one (1145b9–11). The *enkrates* acts in accordance with his judgement; the *akrates* abandons his (b11–13). The *enkrates* knows that his desires are base and resists them; the *akrates* knows that his actions are base but performs them because of his feelings (b13–14). And some people think that the *enkrates* is temperate and the *akrates* intemperate (b15–17).

Having identified the appearances, Aristotle considers some of the problems or puzzles about them. For example, the suggestion that the temperate person is enkratic (1145b15–17) conflicts with the claim that the temperate person's desire for pleasure is neither excessive nor deficient (1119a11–20). The *enkrates*' desire for sense-pleasures, however, is excessive and so he cannot be temperate. Again, the suggestion that the practically wise person could be akratic (1145b18–19) conflicts with the claim that the practically wise person acts on his knowledge, whereas the *akrates* fails to act on his. These puzzles don't present any special difficulties and so I'll simply make a few remarks about the Socratic context of Aristotle's discussion.

Socrates thought that 'knowledge is a fine thing quite capable of ruling a man and that if he can distinguish good from evil, nothing will force him to act otherwise than as knowledge dictates, since wisdom is all the reinforcement he needs' (*Protagoras* 352C). The ground for this claim is the thought that everyone desires what appears to be good (*Meno* 78A; cf. 1113a15–b2 and 1155b25–7). Since everyone desires what appears to be good, the explanation for a person's doing wrong must be that he doesn't *know* what is good. For if he had a correct conception of the good, he would, *ceteris paribus*, perform good actions. This leads Socrates to make the famous claim that 'no one willingly goes to meet evil or what he thinks is evil' (*Protagoras* 358D). As we shall see, there is a respect in which Aristotle thinks Socrates is right. However, contrary to Socrates, Aristotle quite clearly thinks that *akrasia* does exist (1145b28).

VII.3

At the beginning of Chapter 3, Aristotle identifies the issues he is concerned with:

- The sense in which the *akrates* has knowledge or belief (discussed in Chapter 3).
- The sphere of akratic actions (discussed in Chapters 4 and 6).
- The distinction between *akrasia* and intemperance (discussed in Chapters 4 and 7).

In this commentary we will concentrate of the first issue and will make only passing references to the others. Further guidance can be found in the notes to this chapter.[42]

In the present chapter, then, Aristotle presents his positive account of *akrasia* (at 1146b25–1147b19). The precise interpretation of this passage is contentious and so it's a matter of no small importance that we understand the question Aristotle takes himself to be addressing. For if we are unclear about that, his comments are likely to seem confusing. Aristotle claims that 'we must examine whether the *akrates* has knowledge or not, and in what way he has it' (1146b9–10). We could take this matter in two ways:[43]

(i) How can a person fail to perform the best action if he is in full present knowledge of the best action in the circumstances?

(ii) How can a person who fails to perform the best action be said to know what the best action is in the circumstances?

These questions suggest rather different lines of inquiry. Question (i) implies that what needs to be explained is *not* whether, or in what sense, the *akrates* has knowledge of the best action to perform, but rather *how* he manages to do otherwise when in possession of that knowledge. Question (ii), however, implies that what needs to be explained is not *how* the *akrates* performs the wrong action, but whether, and in what sense, he possesses knowledge of the best action to undertake. Matters here are further complicated by other questions the reference to *akrasia* may excite, such as:

(iii) Is it true that a person who judges x better than y and is in a position to do either x or y will do x rather than y?

(iv) Is judging x better than y equivalent to forming an intention to do x rather than y in a situation in which a person will do either x or y?

(v) How is *akrasia* possible?

These are interesting questions, but they are not questions Aristotle's discussion at 1146b25–47a24 addresses. In fact, Aristotle is principally concerned with question (ii). This passage is explicitly concerned with different senses in which a person can be said to know something. But question (i) invites no such discussion because it takes for granted that the *akrates* has 'full present knowledge'. So, Aristotle is trying to specify the sense in which a person who does what is wrong can be said to know, or believe, what is the right action to perform.

Aristotle's first move is to reject one answer to question (ii) that he thinks is obviously false. The answer is that the *akrates* doesn't know *x* is the best thing to do, he only *believes* *x* is the best thing to do; and since, on this view, belief implies a diminished conviction, the person's acting contrary to his belief is explicable: he's not sure that *x* really is the best thing to do. But recourse to the strength of a person's convictions is irrelevant: 'some people's convictions about what they believe are no weaker than other people's convictions about what they know' (1146b30–1). The problem of *akrasia* remains, then, irrespective of a person's acting contrary to knowledge or to belief.

Aristotle evidently thinks a more cogent response to the question can be found in the distinction between two senses in which a person may be said to know something: 'we ascribe [knowledge] both to someone who has it without using it and to someone who is using it' (1146b32–3). It is tempting to put this in the modern idiom of *dispositional* and *occurrent* knowledge. You knew, for example, whether or not you had a shower or a bath or neither this morning before you read this sentence. But this knowledge was dispositional and not occurrent: reading the sentence brought what was dispositional knowledge to mind, making it occurrent. However, Aristotle's point is not just whether knowledge is 'in mind' or not, but whether it is *operative* in the action. It seems entirely possible that a person may have in mind the thought that 'Having sex with my brother's wife is not the best thing for me to do in this situation' while he proceeds to do so. What would be problematic is for that thought to be (partially) causally explanatory of his action. That is to say, a person has sex with his brother's wife *because* he judges it not to be the best thing to do.

The distinction between operative and inoperative knowledge seems to make sense of a range of cases that would otherwise seem extraordinary. For example, I may know that ingesting too much salt is detrimental to my health, but not recall that the dish presented to me in the restaurant is laced with salt (1147a5–8). I may therefore eat the dish, which is contrary, in this sense, to my knowledge. It would, however, be extraordinary for me to eat the dish because it is laced with salt which I know is detrimental to my health.

So far, then, Aristotle has distinguished two senses in which a person can be said to know something. Robinson (1969) thinks that by 1146b36 Aristotle has virtually everything he needs to explain the phenomenon of *akrasia* (p. 80). I think that this is true if we interpret Aristotle according to question (ii). But it's important to note that Aristotle hasn't yet explicitly linked the distinction to the explanation of *akrasia*. He does so in the following passage:

> For we see that having without using includes different types of having; hence some people, such as those asleep or mad or drunk, both have knowledge in a way and do not have it. Moreover, this is the condition of those affected by strong feelings. For spirited reactions, sexual appetites and some conditions of this sort clearly [both disturb knowledge and] disturb the body as well. Clearly, then, [the *akrates*] has knowledge in a way similar to these people. (1147a11–18)

Here Aristotle applies his distinction to a further set of cases (1147a10). A person may have knowledge in the way the unconscious, insane and drunk have knowledge. And this is the sense in which those affected by 'strong feelings' have knowledge too. It's important to note that this is not a new sense in which knowledge may be inoperative; rather it seems to be a sense in which knowledge can be rendered inoperative. Aristotle lists as the causes here 'spirited reactions, sexual appetites and some conditions of this sort'. The claim being made, then, is that when a person is affected by *akrasia* his knowledge is 'disturbed', or rendered inoperative in action, by strong feelings. So, Aristotle's answer to (ii) is that a person's belief that a certain course of action is not the best one to follow is rendered inoperative by strong feelings when he acts akratically.

Aristotle immediately anticipates a potential objection to his answer to question (ii): drunken people, for example, often say things like, 'I really shouldn't have anything more to drink: better make mine a double whisky', and this appears to demonstrate that their knowledge is operative (1147a19–24). Aristotle dismisses this objection on the ground that nothing follows about a person's understanding of what he says from the fact that he utters certain words. In this respect, the *akrates* is similar to an actor who reads his lines without believing them. This response, though, may not receive a sympathetic reception. When the *akrates* does something wrong, knowledge relevant to its wrongness has been rendered inoperative. But is it really credible that in saying 'I shouldn't be doing this' the knowledge or belief that he shouldn't *remains* inoperative? Compare this to the restaurant example above. Surely, if I were to say, 'This dish is laced with salt and I shouldn't eat it', my knowledge that it is laced with salt would be activated. But Aristotle need not be concerned by this objection. Strong feelings are causally responsible for rendering the knowledge of the *akrates* inoperative and only when those feelings have dissipated will the *akrates* have access to it (1147b1–5). Similarly, it is perhaps only when confronted with his sizable hangover that the carouser's knowledge that he shouldn't have yet more to drink will be operative.

Now, if we read 1146b25–47a24 as Aristotle's answer to question (ii), then what are we to make of the difficult passage 1147a25–b19, which follows it? Is it, too, intended as a response to question (ii)? Despite the obscurity of the text, I do not think we find a further sense in which a person acts contrary to what he judges to be the best. A clue about Aristotle's true intentions may be gleaned from his opening remark: 'we may also look at the *cause* in the following way, referring to [human] nature' (1147a25–6; emphasis added). This suggests that he's about to comment on *how* an episode of *akrasia* arises. He is stating what happens in a person affected by *akrasia* and he is not trying to state a new sense in which a person may know something. Given the difficulty of the passage, it is worth having it before us in full:

> Further, we may also look at the cause in the following way, refer-ring to [human] nature. For one belief is universal; the other is about particulars, and because they are particulars, perception controls them. And in the cases where these two beliefs result in one belief, it is necessary, in the one case, for the soul to affirm what has been concluded, but in the case of beliefs about production, to act at once on what has been concluded. If, for

instance, everything sweet must be tasted, and this, some one particular, is sweet, it is necessary for someone who is able and unhin-
dered also to act on this at the same time.

Suppose, then, that someone has the universal belief hindering
him from tasting; he has the second belief, that everything sweet
is pleasant and this is sweet, and this belief is active; but it turns
out that appetite is present in him. The belief, then, [that is formed
from the previous two beliefs] tells him to avoid this, but appetite
leads him on, since it is capable of moving each of the [bodily]
parts. (1147a25–36)

This is a difficult passage and we shan't attempt a full assessment of
it here. But we can make a few comments that will remove some of
its obscurity. Aristotle begins by noting that in theoretical matters
the combination of a universal belief and a particular belief results
in a new belief that the soul affirms. So, for example, if I have the
universal belief that 'a horizontal slab with one or more legs' is a
table, and if, through perception, I have the belief that '*this* is a horizontal slab with four legs', the beliefs combine to form the new
belief '*this* is a table'. In the theoretical case, we recognize this proposition as true. In the practical case, two beliefs may be combined in
a similar way. However, in matters concerned with action, we act on
the conclusion. So, for example, if I have the belief that 'eating pecan
pie is good' and, through perception, the belief that 'this is pecan
pie', the beliefs combine to form the new belief that 'this is good'.
Provided I am able and uninhibited, I will act on this belief and
tuck in.

Given that this is how actions are usually caused, what happens in
cases of *akrasia*? Well, in the instance Aristotle is considering the
person affected by *akrasia* has a universal belief preventing him from
tasting certain kinds of thing. He has another belief that 'everything
sweet is pleasant' and the particular belief that 'this is sweet'. This
particular belief results from the perception of the object, and this
causes universal belief that everything sweet is pleasant to become
operative. Since the person also has a desire for what is pleasant he
is 'led on' and acts contrary to the universal belief that prevents his
tasting the object. The desire in the *akrates* does control his perceptual beliefs in the sense that it causes him to attend to its sweetness as
opposed to its qualities in virtue of which it is not to be tasted. This,
then, is the sense in which the Socratic account is correct: perceptual

knowledge may be dragged about, but not knowledge of goodness (1147b16–18).

So, Aristotle specifies the sense in which a person who does what is bad knows what is best. He likens the condition to a drunken episode and tries to show how the knowledge the *akrates* has leads to his acting as he does. The account confirms that Socrates was wrong to say there is no such thing as *akrasia*, but right to claim that knowledge of a certain kind cannot be overpowered by desire.

There are, however, some outstanding issues. Firstly, we have not yet had explained to us how the *akrates'* desire for what is pleasant takes precedence over the 'universal' belief that it is not to be tasted. We will consider the implications of this problem in the next section. And secondly, it is not clear that the *akrates'* perceptual knowledge is 'dragged about' because it is operative in action and it seems that the *akrates'* universal knowledge (that this shouldn't be tasted) is 'dragged out' (i.e. rendered inoperative).

VII.4–10

Aristotle claims that there is *akrasia* with regard to sense-pleasures and with regard to anger (1148a17; 1149a25). He claims that *akrasia* about sense-pleasure is more shameful than *akrasia* about anger because, in the latter, reason and reflection play some role (1149b1–4). The point is that for a person to get angry, appropriately or otherwise, he must deploy concepts of fairness and self-respect in his assessment of his circumstances. Such a process of assessment is characteristic of *human* activity. But the desire for sensory gratification does not imply reasoning characteristic of human beings. So, *akrasia* about sense-pleasure is closer to the bestial level and so more shameful (cf. 1118a25–7).

Donald Davidson points out that on Aristotle's account it's not obvious that *akrasia* is a blameworthy condition (p. 35). As Davidson construes Aristotle here, there are in the soul two competing aspects, 'reason' and 'passion', and it just so happens that passion wins. But in what sense could the agent have done anything about the victor? As we have seen, Aristotle thinks that the feelings we have are dependent on character. He also thinks that we are responsible for the character we have. So, for Aristotle, to the extent that the *akrates* has excessive desires he is culpable even if, now that he has them, he finds it difficult to 'resist' them. This response to Davidson is not entirely satisfactory because Aristotle is very clear that the *akrates*, unlike the intemperate, is curable (1151a13–14). The *akrates* is not persuaded that the pursuit of excessive sense-pleasure is best and so he can be 'talked out of it'. But we might think Aristotle has got matters confused here. After all, reason proves itself ineffective in the *akrates* in its role of regulating desires; whereas it is effective in the vicious person. The vicious person exercises reason effectively but with a mistaken conception of the good.

Finally, Aristotle account of *akrasia* is sometimes thought not to represent accurately the phenomenology of the experience of it. When we are affected by *akrasia*, it is said that we may be thinking 'Eating this cake is bad for me' when we do so. But Aristotle thinks that thoughts with such content are not available until *after* the akratic episode. It is for precisely this reason that I have stressed Aristotle's remark that it's not just whether the thought is available but whether it is part of the explanation of the action. So, on this account, at least, Aristotle's view is consistent with the popular account of the experience's phenomenology. This brings our discussion of *akrasia* to a close: we have skated quickly over many issues, but the reader will find references in the notes to follow up interpretations and objections.[44]

VII.11–14

It is appropriate to have a discussion of the goodness of pleasure after the discussion of *akrasia* because that discussion may have given the impression that pleasure is bad because it leads us astray (cf. 1104b10). So, it is fitting for Aristotle to lock horns with some of the arguments for the conclusion that pleasure is bad. Although this is true, it's not clear that Aristotle had such an intention. In his stated motivation for discussing pleasure he claims it necessary because (a) pleasure and pain are the proper subjects of study for political philosophy and (b) virtue and vice are concerned with pleasure and so we must have an account of pleasure (1152b1–6).

Aristotle notes three negative views held with regard to pleasure:

(1) Pleasure is not good.
(2) Some pleasures are good, but most are bad.
(3) Even if all pleasures are good, the supreme good is not pleasure.

He goes on to note arguments for each of these claims. The conclusion (1) that pleasure is not good is inferred from several premises: (i) pleasure is process and processes are not goods; (ii) temperate people are good and they avoid pleasure; and (iii) pleasure impedes practical reasoning. The alleged existence of despicable pleasures is supposed to support (2). And since the supreme good is an end, not a process, conclusion (3) also follows from premise (i).

In Chapter 12 Aristotle argues that none of the arguments for (1) to (3) are sound. Against (i) he claims that goodness is spoken of in two ways: good without qualification and good for some particular person (1152b26–7). Since some processes are good for a particular person at a particular time, it is not true to claim that no processes are good. Against (2) he claims that the temperate person does not avoid every pleasure: for there is a proper way to enjoy sense-pleasures. Against (3) Aristotle argues that pleasures are not processes. This last claim merits closer attention.

One way of construing pleasure is as the process of relieving some pain or lack. On this model a person perceives something about his circumstances as in some way deficient and seeks to ameliorate it. Pleasure just is the process of rectifying this perceived deficiency. This account is supported by reflection on certain bodily pleasures. When I feel thirsty, for example, I perceive the need for a drink. The experience of slaking my thirst is pleasurable as I return to a state in which I perceive no further need for refreshment. Aristotle thinks all this quite wrong: 'pleasures are not [processes] . . . they are activities and an end [in themselves] and arise when we exercise [a capacity] . . . of the natural state . . . unimpeded' (1153a10–14). So, pleasure, on this account, is an unimpeded activity of the natural state. But what precisely does this mean? Consider the activity of sawing some wood. Aristotle seems to think that this will be pleasurable provided it is not impeded in some way. Impediments to this activity might include: an inappropriate saw (perhaps it's very blunt); an excitable child who keeps tugging at your sawing hand; or a strong desire not to be sawing but watching TV. If the sawing is free from such impediments, it will be pleasurable.

What is not entirely clear is whether Aristotle intends his remarks in Chapter 12 to capture his *entire* theory of pleasure. They appear in a section the explicit purpose of which is the rebuttal of arguments for conclusions (1) to (3). Some commentators, however, suggest that Aristotle argues for the positive conclusion that the supreme good is a pleasure, on the basis that the supreme good is an activity and, if unimpeded, is a pleasure (see, for example, Bostock, p. 144). This seems to me to press the text too far. Throughout the relevant section 1153b6–18, which is cited in support of this inter-pretation, Aristotle refers to what 'all [people] think' and what 'plea-sure might be'. These qualifications are not insignificant for they suggest that Aristotle by drawing our attention to intuitions that conflict with that argument, is trying to establish that the argument for (3) is not sound.

In Chapter 14 Aristotle explains the falsity of the view that bodily pleasures are the more choice-worthy. I will not review his arguments here. However, I will return to these themes in my assessment of *NE* X.1–5, which is generally regarded as representing Aristotle's posi-tive view of pleasure.[45]

Study questions

1. What reasons are there for thinking the virtuous person is more impressive than the *enkrates* who has to fight against his desires?
2. Given the scope of Aristotle's interest in the problem of *akrasia*, is there any value in his account of it?
3. Why does the desire for sensory pleasure defeat the universal judgement of the *akrates*?
4. Why does Aristotle discuss pleasure?
5. What is Aristotle's positive account of pleasure?

NE VIII–IX

Introduction

Having completed his discussions of *akrasia* and pleasure, Aristotle considers friendship. The importance he attaches to the subject is immediately apparent from his dedicating two of the ten books of the *NE* to an examination of its nature and proper place in a *eudai-mon* life.[46] And the importance he attaches to it is not, in my view, misplaced, because friendship is a central phenomenon in human life. What we find in *NE* VIII–IX is some of the most profound, fas-cinating and insightful material of the entire treatise. It illuminates not just the nature of friendship itself, but also the true motivation and goodness of active beneficence and the indispensability of friends in a good and worthwhile life.

A complete examination of Aristotle's discussion is well beyond the scope of the present commentary. We could easily devote a full-length book to it, as indeed others already have (and very successfully:

see, for example, Price 1989 and Pakaluk 1980). Our discussion will concentrate first on the three types of friendship Aristotle identifies in *NE* VIII.3 and the ground he offers for taking one of these to be the primary case of friendship, the others being derived from it. It is natural to follow this with some brief remarks about the different kinds of activity characteristic of the types of friendship, and so we'll examine *NE* VIII.5–6. We will then examine the nature and problem of self-love and will conclude with some brief remarks about the place of friendship in a *eudaimon* life. This inevitably leaves much of the material untouched. This should not be taken as implying that there is nothing of value in the chapters I've omitted. It is merely to attempt as full a discussion as possible of material most pertinent to our approach to understanding the best lives for human beings and the place of friendship in such lives.

Before we begin we should note the translation. 'Friendship' is generally considered the best rendering of the Greek *'philia'*, though the English lacks the corresponding verb form *'philein'*, which is usually translated 'to love'. One disadvantage of this is that the English term 'friendship' is narrower in connotation than *'philia'*. The English term, for example, does not cover the relationships we have with business associates, colleagues and shop assistants: we wouldn't automatically characterize the relationship between a retailer and a wholesaler as a friendship. This is because the English term implies a certain degree of intimacy and familiarity that is not present in the Greek. Indeed, the relationship between wholesaler and retailer would fall under the extension of the Greek term *'philia'*. Although elsewhere in this commentary I have used the Greek terms, I will here continue to use the English term 'friendship' because it captures those aspects of mutuality, concern and activity that Aristotle attributes to the 'primary case' of *'philia'*.

VIII.1

Aristotle begins by motivating the entire discussion. He claims we should discuss friendship because 'it is a virtue or it involves virtue' (1155a4). To say that friendship is a virtue sounds very strange, not least because it's not at all clear how friendship could fit into the pattern of the virtues characterized at *NE* II.6. Aristotle certainly regards friendship as a good: in fact he thinks complete friendship is *the* 'greatest external good' (1169b11). But, of course, there are many things that Aristotle regards as good, such as money, that are not virtues. Perhaps, then, all that is meant here is that friendship *implies* virtue because 'complete friendship' is friendship between two persons of equal virtue (1156b7ff.).

Having noted the connection between virtue and friendship, Aristotle immediately provides a further reason for his inquiry: '[friendship] is most necessary for life' (1155a5). He substantiates this 'appearance' with a list of common beliefs about friendship. For example, a person who had all the other goods wouldn't choose to live without friends (1155a6). Again, a person only seems to benefit from prosperity if he has the opportunity to act beneficently (1155a8–10). And finally, in poverty and infirmity, friends seem the only refuge (1155a11–12). These beliefs indicate the place and significance of friendship in life and provide initial grounds for our studying it. But there are a number of puzzles the common beliefs evoke:

1. Is it true that friendship implies a similarity between the parties or is it the case that 'opposites attract' (1155a34–7)?
2. Does friendship arise between all sorts of people or can certain sorts of people, the vicious, not be friends (1155b11–12)?
3. Is there just one type of friendship or many kinds (1155b12–13)?

In the course of his discussion Aristotle's responses to these puzzles emerge: puzzles (1) and (2) are clarified in *NE* VIII.4; and puzzle (3) is considered immediately in *NE* VIII.2–3.

VIII.2

Aristotle thinks that we can determine whether there is one or more type of friendship by first examining what we find lovable (1155b17). The idea seems to be this: once we have identified what people love in one another, we can consider whether all types of loving satisfy the criteria for friendship or not. We may wonder, though, why Aristotle begins by considering love and the causes of love. Here we should recall that 'love' translates the verb '*philein*' for which there is no direct English equivalent. Aristotle is assuming that friends stand in some relation to one another and is examining the different possible bases for such a relation.

Let's begin by considering Aristotle's conception of love. A person P loves some x if, and only if, P perceives x as good for P (1155b25–6). It follows from this definition that a person may equally love both animate and inanimate objects. I may perceive oranges as being good for me and so, on Aristotle's definition, may be said to love oranges. I may also perceive a carpenter as good for me, especially when I want a fence constructed, and so be said to love my carpenter. Aristotle claims that there are three causes of love: the good, the pleasant and the useful (1155b19). However, since we only love the useful because it procures for us what is either good or pleasant, the *ends* we love are the good and the pleasant (1155b21).

Having specified his conception of love, Aristotle presents formal criteria for friendship. He begins by noting that love for what is inanimate is not friendship for, while a person may love chocolate we certainly wouldn't say he was friends with it (1155b26–7). The explanation for this is that friendship implies wishing good for the other and since we don't wish good for a bar of chocolate, it follows that the person and the bar of chocolate are not friends (1155b31–2). Aristotle claims that in wishing good for another person, we are said to have good will for him (1155b32). However, merely having good will for another person is to be distinguished from friendship for two reasons. Firstly, a person may have good will for another, but since the other doesn't have good will for him they are not friends: friendship implies *reciprocated* good will (1155b34). Secondly, two people may have good will for one another but be unaware that they do (1155b35–1156a4). They may not have met, for instance; but, were they to meet and become aware of their mutual good will, then we would describe them as friends. To sum up: A and B are friends if and only if A and B (i) love one another because of 'one of the causes mentioned above' (1156a6); (ii) wish good for one another for each other's sake; and (iii) are both aware of this mutual and reciprocated good will. Condition (i) here is ambiguous. It could mean that A and B must love one another for utility, pleasure or goodness; or it could mean that A and B must love one another for only *one* of these causes, e.g. goodness. The text appears to imply the latter of these interpretations.

VIII.3

Aristotle initially states that there are three species of friendship because there are three types of loving (1156a7–8): friends because of utility; friends because of pleasure; and friends because of goodness. Before we consider Aristotle's remarks about these varieties of friendship we should consider in a little more depth what kind of a relationship Aristotle has in mind in each case. If A and B are friends because of utility, then both A and B recognize the other as having something they perceive to be useful for themselves and this is the basis of their friendship. For example, my relationship with a taxi driver: he has something I want, *viz* the capacity to get me home; and I have something he wants, *viz* money.[47] If A and B are friends because of pleasure, then B causes A pleasure and A causes B pleasure and this is the basis of their friendship. For example, two people who find each other witty or amusing company: they both bring the other pleasure. And finally, if A and B are friends because of goodness, then both recognize the other as virtuous and this is the basis of their relationship.

We should not, however, assume that these three types of loving satisfy the criteria for friendship specified in *NE* VIII.2. In particular, it is not clear that Aristotle thinks friendships based on utility and pleasure satisfy conditions (ii) and (iii). He writes:

> Those who love each other wish goods to each other insofar as they love each other. Those who love each other for utility love the other *not in his own right* but only insofar as they gain some good for themselves from him. The same is true of those who love for pleasure; for they like a witty person not because of his character but because he is pleasant to them. (1156a9–14; emphasis added)

It is on this basis that Aristotle describes these lovable characteristics as 'coincidental' (1156a18). To the person who loves another for pleasure, it is the pleasure, and not the other person who happens to be pleasant, that he loves. To him, it doesn't really matter *who* is pleasant, just so long as *someone* is. It is, of course, possible that a person offers a distinctive kind of pleasure so that just anyone won't do: but nonetheless there is mere coincidence between the kind of pleasure I love and the kind that the person I love gives me. And the same goes for utility: what I want is my car fixed and I will have good will for *whoever* can fix it. There is, then, a coincidence in both cases between what A perceives as pleasant or useful for himself at a certain point in time and what B can provide him with and vice versa.

It seems, then, that so-called friendships for pleasure or utility are not really friendships at all because they fail to satisfy condition (ii), which makes it impossible for them to satisfy (iii). In neither case do A and B wish each other goods for each other's sake, but only insofar as the other delivers what is pleasant or useful. Should either A or B cease to deliver what is pleasant or useful to the other, the so-called friendship would be dissolved (1156a20–2; though cf. 1165b13–15). This seems to imply that relationships based on pleasure or utility aren't actually friendships at all.

Matters are apparently quite different when it comes to 'complete friendship': friendship found among people similar in virtue. 'They wish goods in the same way to one another insofar as they are good, and they are good in their own right' (1156b8–9). These relationships are *not* coincidental: a person is not loved because he gives pleasure or because he is useful; he is loved because of his virtuous character. As a consequence, such relationships endure (though not necessarily forever) because a virtuous state of character endures (1156b11–12). A further consequence is that such friends will also be useful and pleasant to one another because they are themselves good without qualification. They will be useful because they will contribute to each other's good and they will be pleasant because they act in accordance with virtue and a good person will take pleasure in his friend's virtuous actions (cf. 1170a1–4). 'Hence loving and friendship are found most of all and at their best in these friends' (1156b24). This suggests that only friends of similar virtue are actually friends, and other relationships are called friendships because of some resemblance they bear to the primary case (1156b34–1157a3). John Cooper (1975) dramatically sums up this interpretation:

> It should be observed that if Aristotle holds that both pleasure- and advantage-friends are wholly self-centred and that only perfectly virtuous persons are capable of having relationships of any other type, he will be adopting an extremely harsh view of the psychological capabilities of almost everyone . . . this would be a depressing result. (p. 305)[48]

The worry is this: in stating that only persons of virtue can be friends Aristotle sets the requirements for friendship so high that hardly any relationships will qualify (cf. 1156b25–6). This is because virtue itself is something difficult to achieve. If only the virtuous have friends, then, contrary to what we might think, few of us actually enjoy friendships. Cooper's own response to this problem is to interpret Aristotle as understanding friendship based on virtue as friendship based on character. Two people can love one another on account of their respective characters even if they are not virtuous, but are perhaps 'on the road' to virtue (p. 308). It is certainly true that Aristotle seems to have neglected the possibility that two people could love one another because of their respective characters and indeed their personalities even if neither of them is virtuous (cf. Annas 1977, p. 549).[49] We might recall in this connection Montaigne's remark about his friend Étienne de la Boétie: 'If I am pressed to say why I loved him, I feel it can only be explained by replying: "Because it was he; because it was me" ' (*Essays*, Bk. 1, Ch. 28, 'On friendship'). However, it is another matter whether Aristotle intended this apparently neglected possibility to be part of his characterization of friendship based on goodness.

The question remains, then, whether according to Aristotle there is one or more type of friendship. It is quite clear that there is *some* distinction to be drawn between the different types of friendship (1156b34–1157a3). Quite whether that implies friendship is something seldom realized depends on our interpretation of the text. Is it true that, unlike friendships based on virtue, friendships based on pleasure or utility do not satisfy conditions (ii) and (iii)?

The suspicion that neither friendships based on pleasure nor those based on utility satisfy condition (ii) is due to Aristotle's explicit claim that such friends wish good for each other only to the extent that they derive pleasure or utility from one another and not *because of* each other (1156a15–19). There is certainly a dependency between wishing good for a person and that person's being perceived as lovable in some way by the person who loves him. But this is true too of friendship based on goodness. If a person were to cease to be good, his friend may cease to love him and would no longer wish him goods. Aristotle entertains a possibility like this when he considers a person who tricked us into thinking he was virtuous, when in fact he was not (1165b13–15; cf. 1156b12). But perhaps this misses the point: the reason why friendships based on utility or pleasure fail to satisfy condition (ii) is because they are really self-interested (1167a14–18). But Aristotle claims that the virtuous person loves himself most of all and his definition of love at 1155b22–7 explicitly states that a person loves another he perceives as being *good for himself* (cf. 1168b29–30). Only some varieties of self-love are to be condemned and nothing in *NE* VIII.3 implies that all relationships based on utility or pleasure exhibit the kind of self-love condemned in *NE* IX.8.

The true difference between friendships based on goodness and those based on pleasure or utility lies in Aristotle's remark that the latter two are 'coincidental'. Person A is only loved (e.g. for utility) by person B because B recognizes that A is in some way useful to him. If B did not happen to have a desire for that use, he would not love A. In this instance, A is lovable *but only to the extent* that B has this particular desire. In friendships based on goodness, however, both people are lovable *without qualification*. They are worthy of our love apart from any desires we might have, which is why Aristotle wants to say that we love such a person for himself. It is, of course, true that if I am not a good person myself I may not recognize a good person as being worthy of love, but it doesn't follow that he is not lovable: 'For the absolutely good is absolutely desirable, but for each individual his own [perceived good is desirable]' (*EE* 1237a1–2). Aristotle's point, then, is that a good person is worthy of love without qualification. However, a person who is loved for his utility is only loved to the extent that another has a desire for what is useful and so is not loved without qualification. This also explains why Aristotle does not appear to have included all character-based relationships. It is because there is only one kind of character that is absolutely lovable: the character of the virtuous person.

So, according to Aristotle the primary case of friendship, which is referred to as *complete friendship*, is that between people of equal virtue. Only in such friendships are both parties lovable without qualification. Friendships based on pleasure or utility resemble the primary case to the extent that the parties wish good for each other. However, people who are loved for pleasure or utility are only loved to the extent that others desire their pleasure or what they are useful for.

VIII.5–6

The central claim of Chapter 5 is that friendship, like virtue, is essentially active. Two people who are aware of mutual good will between them may cease to be friends if they are absent from one another for a long time because they will be unable to fully express their friendship in the way proper to mutual good will (1157b10–14). We may, of course, be pleased to meet people we used to know at a reunion, but the experience has a very different character from the experience of interacting with friends we see more frequently. This is not to say such relationships cannot be rekindled; just that at the moment of reunion it is not in such a state. Aristotle goes on to stress that 'living together is [most] proper to friendship' (1157b20–1). This is likely to strike the modern reader with surprise. However, he does not mean that people should, as we would say, 'move in together' and occupy the same residence. Rather, he has in mind shared experiences, conversation and activity (cf. *NE* IX.9).

In Chapter 6 Aristotle identifies other features characteristic of the different types of friendship. For example, one person cannot have complete friendship with many people (1158a11). This is not just because of the scarcity of people of complete virtue, but also because of the time it takes for such a relationship to emerge: 'for though the wish for friendship comes quickly, friendship does not' (1156b33). However, it is possible for a person to have many friendships for utility or pleasure both because the incidence of such people is greater and the 'services take little time' (1158a16–17). For example, I don't have to be familiar with my mechanic to get him to fix my car. We both recognize what we want from one another and can immediately seek our respective goals.

However, friendships for utility differ in this respect from friendships for pleasure or for good. The goals sought in friendships for utility are typically different: I seek a working car; my mechanic seeks payment. In friendships for pleasure or for the good, the same thing is sought by both people: respectively, pleasure or goodness. The final point to note here is that although in friendship people do not always receive what they give, as in relationships of utility, in general friendship is characterized in terms of parity: friends wish good for the other and receive in return something of equal value. This concludes our discussion of *NE* VIII. In the remaining chapters Aristotle considers, among other things, friendships in communities and families.

IX.4

Book IX begins with the consideration of friendships in which people have different aims and the dissolution of such friendships. Following this Aristotle turns to the relationship between friendship towards others and friendship towards oneself. This passage of the *NE* is traditionally examined in terms of its contribution to the debate about 'egoism and altruism': the concern being that, according to Aristotle, *all* relationships are ultimately egoistic. However, Aristotle's principal interest in this chapter is the *origin* of friendship: 'the defining features of friendship that are found in friendships to one's neighbours would seem to be derived from features of friendship towards oneself' (1166a1–3).

Aristotle's strategy is to identify five characteristics of friendship and then to argue that these are present most of all in a person's relationship to himself. Friendship is, then, naturally interpreted as an extension of the relationship a person has with himself to others. The five features of friendship are: (1) a friend wishes and does good for his friend's sake (2) a friend wishes his friend to be and live for his own sake (3) a friend spends time with his friend; (4) friends make the same choices; and (5) friends share in one another's joys and distresses (1166a3–9). Aristotle then states that these features are 'found in the decent person's relation to himself' (1166a10). So, a good person wishes, and does, what is good for himself (1). He wishes to live and to continue to live as himself and not another person (2). A good person wishes to spend time by himself and enjoys doing so (3). The choices of the good person exhibit harmony between the rational and the non-rational parts of the soul (4). He shares his distresses and his pleasures (5).

But we might be sceptical about the alleged argument for the claim that starts the chapter. Even if it's true that friendship between good persons is formally equivalent to the relationship a person has with himself, it doesn't follow that the latter is the cause of the former. Bostock suggests that Aristotle may have meant that friendship towards oneself *explains* friendship towards others (pp. 174–5). On this account, the reason for one person's loving another is his loving himself. However, even this alternative interpretation is not implied by the text, as Bostock himself acknowledges. Perhaps Aristotle's true concern here is just to show that in friendship two people carry over the concern they have for themselves to each other and that this can be seen from the presence in each case of the characteristics identified. Just as I will seek to protect my person and my property, so will I seek to protect my friend and his property.

Aristotle then raises the question as to whether there is friendship towards oneself or not (1166a34; cf. *NE* V.11). He notes that the possibility of a person's being a friend to himself implies the presence of separable parts (1166a35–6). These are the parts of the soul Aristotle originally distinguished at *NE* I.13: the part of the soul without, but obedient to, reason; and the part of the soul with reason. In the good person these parts of the soul act in harmony: the part of the soul obedient to reason desires that goal that the part of the soul with reason judges to be best. In a bad person, Aristotle tells us, there is no such harmony: the person is at odds with himself (1166b6). So, in a sense there is something analogous to friendship between persons within a person's soul.

There are outstanding matters of interpretation. Firstly, there is disquiet about the sense that can be made of the idea that a friend is 'another self' on the logical ground that a person cannot, for example, have another's pain (Annas 1977, p. 542). Secondly, there is a charge of inconsistency with regard to the account of disharmony between the parts of the soul in the bad person. Elsewhere in the *NE* it is the *enkrates* and *akrates*, and not the vicious, who are said to be conflicted in the sense described in the previous paragraph. And thirdly, there is enduring uneasiness about the claim that self-love is, in some sense at least, good. We will return to the last of these matters, which I take to be the most significant for the *NE* overall, in our discussion of *NE* IX.8.

IX.7

Aristotle has claimed that friends wish good for each other. The discussion of self-love from *NE* IX.4 has raised the matter of the motivation of the virtuous person in his actions: does he act for the sake of the other or for his own sake? We begin to get some sense of Aristotle's answer to this question by his examination of the character of active beneficence.

Aristotle begins by noting that the relationship between a benefactor and his beneficiary is sometimes likened to that of creditor and debtor. The relationship of creditor and debtor is not symmetrical: the creditor wishes the debtor well whereas the debtor wishes the creditor didn't exist (1167618–25). As it happens, Aristotle himself doesn't think this quite true. The creditor doesn't really wish the debtor well, he wishes for repayment of the loan and interest. But if this characterization of the relationship between the benefactor and beneficiary is in all other respects correct, we should expect to find benefactors wanting to receive something from their beneficiaries and beneficiaries simply wishing their benefactors didn't exist. This is not what we find: Aristotle claims on the contrary that the benefactors love their beneficiaries even if they are of little present or future use to them. Furthermore, beneficiaries appreciate their benefactors as those who provide for them some advantage. On these grounds Aristotle rejects the likening of benefactors and beneficiaries to creditors and debtors.

It is worth noting, though, how prevalent the concepts of credit and debt are among people's understanding of relationships even today. One instance in which this is particularly clear is in our practices of making gifts to one another. Sometimes people seem almost to *resent* receiving a gift because of the (perceived) implication that they now *owe* a gift in return. If nothing else, this reveals the extent to which economic and legal concepts colour our interpersonal relationships.

Returning to the text, Aristotle's preferred analogy here is between the producer (benefactor) and the product (beneficiary). The producer loves his product more than his product would love him (were it ensouled). It is worth noting in this context *NE* VIII.8 where Aristotle argues that giving and loving are more proper to friendship than receiving and being loved. We can learn much about the structure of this relationship from the following comments:

> The reason for [the producer's loving his product more than it loves him] is that being is choice-worthy and lovable for all, and we are insofar as we are actualised, since we are insofar as we live and act. Now the product is, in a way, the producer in his actualisation; hence the producer is fond of the product because he loves his own being. This is natural since what he is in potentiality is what the product indicates in actualisation. (1168a6–9)

In acting beneficently, a person *actualizes* himself and 'sees' in his beneficent action his own being actualized. This is a curious statement, but we can perhaps grasp Aristotle's meaning by examining the following personal example. A few years ago I was waiting at a bus stop in Dunedin, New Zealand. I had with me two very large (and heavy) bags and a tent. The timetable helpfully informed travellers that buses served the route but specified no times whatsoever. I had been waiting for about two hours when, to my surprise, a car pulled over despite my not having thumbed for a lift. The driver, a man in his early seventies, asked me if I needed a lift anywhere. I said I was heading to the station and he kindly offered to drive me. He insisted I get into the front seat of his car while *he* went to the bus shelter to retrieve my bags and put them in the boot of his car. When he dropped me off, he once again insisted on carrying my bags to the station entrance before bidding me farewell. It was a good thing that happened. Aristotle's point is that in helping me get to the station, the resident of Dunedin realized his potential and, since we *are* to the extent that we realize our potential, he was (I hope) presently alive to himself (cf. Dent 1988, p. 131 for an excellent statement of this).

However, this structure appears to be present in malign relations too. For do I not, in humiliating another person, actualize my potential and thereby appear to myself more fully and completely alive? This is an unsettling possibility and one that we will return to having outlined Aristotle's distinction between self-love and selfishness in the next chapter.

IX.8

Aristotle's account of the nature of beneficence may have left the reader with the impression that, as his critics allege, the ultimate basis of action is wholly self-interested. Although superficially a person may perform a generous action, this is a mere façade for in acting at all he is merely savouring the pleasure of his own vital existence. Consider Hume's characteristically forceful presentation:

> This [is the view] that all *benevolence* is mere hypocrisy, friendship a cheat, public spirit a farce, fidelity a snare to procure trust and confidence; and that, while all of us at bottom pursue only our private interest, we wear these fair disguises in order to put others off their guard and expose them more to our wiles and machinations. (1751 [1983] Appendix II; cf. Butler 'Sermon XI')

Although Aristotle thinks it's true that we love ourselves most of all (and all the more so the more virtuous we are), he would, with Hume, reject this depressing picture of our interpersonal relationships.

Aristotle begins by characterizing the appearances of the opposing positions on this issue. One view has it that the base do everything for the sake of themselves and indeed will go to any length to secure what they want and would never 'put themselves out' for the sake of others (1168a32–3). The virtuous and decent, on this view, act solely for the sake of the fine and all the more so the better they are, sparing little or no thought for their own interests. This account suggests that only the base act for their own sake, whereas the virtuous act for the sake of others or for the sake of 'the fine'. The other view has it that we must reserve the greatest love for the person who is most a friend. Aristotle has already argued in *NE* IX.4 that we are friends most of all to ourselves and from this it follows that we must love ourselves most of all. This then is the problem concerning self-love.

To resolve this difficulty Aristotle tries to characterize that form of self-love that is generally thought to be deplorable. He thinks it reasonably obvious that people are reproached when they award themselves the biggest share of money, honour or bodily pleasure to the detriment of others' shares (1168b17ff.). Aristotle claims that in acting like this people gratify the non-rational part of the soul and its appetites. These people are given the name 'self-lovers' and are rightly condemned (1168b23).

Aristotle then asks us to consider a person who habitually seeks to do what is right and proper and who is generous, kind and brave: surely no one would call him a self-lover in the sense developed in the previous paragraph (1168b25–8). But, Aristotle points out, this second person seems to be *more* of a self-lover than the first person (1168b29–31). He gives two reasons for this. Firstly, this person awards himself what is best: this is the fine, for the sake of which the virtuous person has acted. Secondly, this person gratifies the rational part of his soul and, since this is finest part of himself, he gratifies the best part of himself.

On what basis, then, may we distinguish the two sorts of person? Aristotle's thought seems to be this. The virtuous person acts on the basis of reason and not appetite and as such he acts in a way that reflects the true value of the options available to him. The base person, however, acts on the appetites that present themselves and as such has little or no order in his life. Although a base person may aim at loving himself, he fails to do this because he harms both himself and others (1169a13–14).

Aristotle thinks that in the terms described above we can make sense of self-sacrifice (1169a26ff.). The prospect of giving up one's life seems to conflict with the thought that we love ourselves most of all – a thought that suggests we would strive to keep ourselves alive at any cost. But consider the following example: a person walks home with his partner when they are confronted by armed assailants. The person could run and leave his partner to fend for himself and in doing so might escape with his life. But he would also escape with the knowledge that he left the person he loved in jeopardy. This would not be a fine (*kalon*) thing to do and so he would have failed to award himself what is best. However, let's suppose that in protecting his lover, the person was murdered. This is a tragedy: a fine and worthwhile life cut short unnecessarily by the greed, or whatever, of others. Although such a person is not *athlios* or miserable, for he has not done what is vicious, nor can he be *eudaimon* because he has suffered misfortune (1100b35ff.). Aristotle certainly thinks that acting for the sake of the fine may, on some occasions at least, be harmful to us (1117a33–b23). Nonetheless, it is only in acting for the sake of the fine that any of us stands a chance of being good (1105b12): deprived of this motive, a person's actions lose the characteristic that gives them their worth.

IX.9

Some of Aristotle's earlier comments may have given rise to the erroneous thought that the *eudaimon* person has no need of friends. After all he is, *ex hypothesi*, in the possession of all the goods and is self-sufficient, so in what way could he be in want of friends? Aristotle rejects this line of thought as absurd (1169b9). He gives three reasons for thinking that friendship is necessary for a *eudaimon* life. Firstly, friends are the greatest external good and it would be ridiculous for a person to have all the goods and not to have the greatest external good (1169b9–11). Secondly, since it is more proper to confer goods than to receive them, then the virtuous person will need friends upon whom to confer goods (1169b11–13). And thirdly, no one would choose to have the other goods and live alone, nor would one choose to share one's days with strangers, and so the *eudaimon* person needs friends (1169b17–22).

However, Aristotle evidently does not think the three arguments developed in the previous paragraph are sufficient. He goes on to develop some intriguing though puzzling arguments in support of his conclusion that a *eudaimon* life includes friendship.

The first argument is contained in the passage at 1169b29–1170a4. Aristotle begins by recalling that a *eudaimon* life is an active, excellent life and we are, as such, lovers of what is good. Since we are better able to observe our neighbour's action than our own, it follows that we will be better able to observe the goodness in our neighbour's action than our own.[50] Since a virtuous person is a 'lover of the fine' he will be attracted to the virtuous actions of others and will take pleasure in observing them (cf. Gore Vidal's striking comment that 'whenever a friend succeeds a little something in me dies' (*The Sunday Times*, 16 September 1973)). To the extent that he is better able to observe virtue in others than in himself he will require friends to observe. There is no denying, however, the obscurity of this argument: for it is not clear how this amounts to a *requirement* for the virtuous person to live a complete and full life as opposed to a preference.

The second argument is at 1170a5–10. Aristotle claims that a solitary person's life is hard because it is difficult to maintain continuous activity alone. It is, however, far easier to maintain it in the company of others with a similar virtuous nature. Therefore, we are more likely to be continuously virtuous if we are surrounded by like-minded people who buoy us up in difficult times. It must be said that this passage seems to diminish the status of the *eudaimon* person who has elsewhere been characterized as the acme of human achievement.

The final argument at 1170a13–b19 is perhaps the most obscure of all. In it Aristotle argues for the following conclusion: 'an excellent friend would seem to be choice-worthy by nature for an excellent person'. He establishes this on the following grounds. Life is in itself good and pleasant: something that can be seen from the fact that everyone desires it. To live is to perceive and to understand and in perceiving and understanding we are aware of ourselves as perceiving and understanding. To perceive that we are alive is pleasant in itself because we perceive in ourselves what is good. Therefore, life itself is choice-worthy. Since an excellent person is related to himself as he is to his friends, his friend's life is choice-worthy in the same way. In living together (sharing thought and conversation) the excellent person and his friend will perceive what is good. That is to say, they will perceive their perception and understanding which is equivalent to their perception of themselves as living beings. It is, then, choice-worthy for a person to live with an excellent friend and since a *eudaimon* life is self-sufficient (i.e. lacking in nothing), a *eudaimon* person cannot be without what is choice-worthy. Therefore, a *eudaimon* person must have excellent friends.

This is a complex argument and this is not the place to attempt a full assessment of it. I see in this the full expression of the point we considered in *NE* IX.7 regarding the character of active beneficence. We also see the beginnings of a response to the problem we raised in our discussion of that passage: *viz* that the base person can realize his being in his deplorable actions. Aristotle claims that a base life is lacking in order because it is characteristic of the base person to over- or under-estimate the importance of some good in the context of life. The experience of such a life will not be good precisely because it will be painful to the person who lives it. Consider, for example, the irascible person (*NE* IV.5): he is apt to see himself as the victim of unwarranted injury more than is actually the case. As such he will experience himself as 'victimized' which is, even to him, a painful condition that is responsible for his ire. He may come to see life as unjust, spiteful, vindictive, and so on. In this he will not experience his perception of life as good. So although a vicious person may, in a sense, realize his being in his actions, he is unlikely to experience this as a good and may represent himself as having to 'fight on all fronts'. Although a (perceived) struggle may invigorate a person, it implies exclusion and isolation, which are not typically felt to be vital or life-confirming.

So, we have considered the varieties of friendship and have isolated complete friendship as a mutually loving relationship between persons of equal virtue. We have further examined the role of friendship in the *eudaimon* life and have considered the character of active beneficence. This leaves us with an enriched understanding both of the best life proper to human beings and of friendship itself. This confirms, in my view, that these books of the *NE* repay particularly close attention.

Study questions

1. In what sense is friendship a virtue?
2. Is there one or more type of friendship?
3. Does friendship often occur?
4. Are all our actions ultimately selfish?
5. Why does the *eudaimon* person need friends?

NE X

Introduction

NE X comprises the second discussion of both pleasure and *eudaimonia*. In our sketch of the account of pleasure in *NE* VII, we suggested that Aristotle's aim was to undermine the (to his mind false) view that pleasure is not good rather than to argue for a positive account of his own. We find a similar attack on the view that pleasure is not the, or a, good in *NE* X. But again, according to some commentators, Aristotle argues for his own positive account: pleasure is an end that supervenes upon an unimpeded activity of the soul. In our discussion we will have to determine whether Aristotle actually intends to present a full theory of his own.

The second analysis of *eudaimonia* is easily stated: it is contemplation (*theoria*). Although easily stated the account presents students of the *NE* with a notoriously difficult matter of interpretation and, despite much scholarly work, the relationship between the account in *NE* I and the account in *NE* X remains problematic. There are two varieties of problem hereabouts: (i) a textual problem concerning the relationship of the texts, their consistency and so on; (ii) a theoretical problem concerning the nature of *eudaimonia* and its title to 'moral goodness' (whatever that is). In our discussion of *NE* X.6–8 we'll first specify the problems and then will consider one solution, though not one that pretends to completeness.

X.1–2

Aristotle's explicit grounds for a discussion of pleasure appear to differ from those at 1152b1–7. There he claimed that (i) pleasure is the proper object of political science; and (ii) pleasure is a component of virtue and in need of further explication. In *NE* X Aristotle reiterates the place of pleasure in virtue but picks up his remarks about the role of pleasure in a good education at 1104b10. However, since the object of political science is the achievement of *eudaimon* lives for the citizens of the community, and since pleasure is a part of virtue, Aristotle is effectively asserting that pleasure is the object of political science. So there does not seem to me any great disparity in his explicit motivation in *NE* X.

Aristotle's first target is a view he attributes to Eudoxus: the view that pleasure is the (supreme) good (1172b10). Although Aristotle records several of Eudoxus' arguments for this conclusion, our discussion will be restricted to two. The first is:

1. All animals (both rational and irrational) seek pleasure.
2. What every animal seeks is the most choice-worthy end.
3. The most choice-worthy end is the supreme good.
∴
4. Pleasure is the supreme good.

Aristotle himself accepts premises (2) and (3) at 1094a1–3, which might suggest that he found Eudoxus' view congenial. However, he clearly rejects (4) and we must consider on what grounds. Aristotle's first move is disappointing: he notes that people accepted Eudoxus' argument because of his 'outstanding temperance' rather than an estimation of his arguments' soundness (1172b17–18). Since he was himself no 'friend of pleasure', people assumed he had no vested interest in the truth of his conclusion and so it *must* be true. All of this may be correct, but it fails to lock horns with the argument presented. Since the argument appears to be valid, the rejection of (4) implies the rejection of one of the premises. As we have said, Aristotle accepts (2) and (3) and so his rejection of the argument implies his rejecting premise (1). Broadie suggests that Aristotle thinks premise (1) is weak because it suggests that pleasure is unified: Aristotle himself thinks pleasures are essentially diverse (1175a21) (Rowe and Broadie 2002, p. 430). So, (1) is false because there is no one thing, pleasure, pursued by all animals.

The second argument we'll examine is rather inscrutable: 'moreover, [Eudoxus argued] when pleasure is added to any other good, to just or temperate actions, for instance, it makes that good more choice-worthy; and good is increased only by the addition of itself' (1172b24–6). What is not clear, however, is just how this is supposed to amount to an argument for the claim that pleasure is the good. Perhaps the thought is this:

(i) The supreme good is self-sufficient: it cannot be improved by the addition of any other good (11097b14–16).

(ii) Pleasure (is the only thing that) cannot be improved by the addition of any other good.

∴

(iii) Therefore, pleasure is the supreme good.

If this is Eudoxus' line of thought, we can make sense of Aristotle's comments that follow: he rejects the claim that pleasure cannot be improved by the addition of any other good (1172b30–2). Aristotle cites Plato who argued in the *Philibus* that pleasure is improved by the addition of practical wisdom (20d–22c). A person who is practically wise will experience the finest pleasures because he correctly judges how best to act. We will leave this survey of Aristotle's response to Eudoxus here and turn to his consideration of the view that pleasure is a process.

X.3

Aristotle's earlier discussion rejected the view that pleasure is a process, but we find a more extensive treatment of that thesis in *NE* X. The argument for the conclusion that pleasure is not the good is:

a. The good is complete.
b. Processes are incomplete.
c. Pleasure is a process.
∴
d. Pleasure is not the good.

The use of the term 'complete' here naturally recalls *NE* I.7. An end is complete if it is sought only for its own sake and not for any further end. Aristotle holds this to be true of the *eudaimonia* and so implicitly accepts (a). A process is undertaken for the sake of some further end: I mix flour and yeast and bake it *for the sake of* producing a loaf of bread. So, it would seem that (b) is true too. Since Aristotle wants to reject (d) he must, therefore, reject (c); and this is just what we find. His strategy is to identify characteristics of processes and demonstrate that they are not characteristics of pleasure. Aristotle claims that processes may be qualified as being quick or slow (1173a34). I may, for example, bake quickly or slowly or I may build a house quickly or slowly. But pleasures may not be qualified as quick or slow, although Aristotle concedes that we may say we become pleased quickly (1173b1). So, Aristotle rejects (c) on the ground that pleasure does not have the same characteristics as processes.

   Although Aristotle considers some further arguments for the claim that pleasure is a process, based on the idea of pleasure as the process of restoration, I won't comment on them further. Instead, we'll briefly consider Aristotle's remarks about disgraceful pleasures and whether they are properly speaking pleasures at all. (This matter was considered in *NE* VII too: see 1152b22–4.) Quite what we should say about this apparent phenomenon is controversial. If we say that such things *are* species of pleasure, then the claim that pleasure is good is false. If we say such things are not species of pleasure at all, then we must account for why certain people pursue them. Aristotle presents his solution to this problem in Chapter 5. Here he notes the different views that may be taken of the so-called despicable pleasures.

Let's begin, though, by noting what sort of pleasures Aristotle has in mind when he refers to disgraceful or despicable pleasures. In doing so we must be careful not to beg any questions, and therefore I put forward examples tentatively. It may be reasonable to think that Aristotle has in mind taking pleasure in such things as eating one's own children or engaging in necrophilia (cf. *NE* VII.5). He presents three potential interpretations of such 'pleasures'. The first is that these are actually not pleasures at all: anybody who appears to take pleasure in such things is mistaken for they are not *really* pleasant. Such acts may appear to be pleasant but only because the person enjoying them is in some bad condition, perhaps owing to disease.[51] The second view is that pleasure is, in itself, choice-worthy but only if it does not originate from shameful sources. The eating of one's children, then, is actually pleasant, but shameful, because the source of the pleasure is shameful. And the third view is that there are different kinds of pleasure, some of which are fine and some of which shameful (1173b22–8). As we shall see, Aristotle's preferred response is the third, but to see this we must examine his account of the value of pleasure in *NE* X.5.

X.4

Aristotle's apparently positive account of pleasure begins with the claim that pleasure is complete at any time in its duration (1174a15). This is a puzzling comment. However, we can make some sense of it by considering the comparative examples Aristotle immediately presents. Take the process of building a house. At any point *during* its building the house is incomplete: it's not true at any time in its construction that the house is built. In fact, it is only true to say this once the *process* of building it has finished. The same is not true of pleasure. At any point during the experience of pleasure it is true to say that the person is pleased or experiencing pleasure. Aristotle introduces a further characteristic of processes not shared by pleasure: processes take time. The thought here is that it takes time to build a house or to bake a loaf of bread; whereas it doesn't take time to be pleased, though we may say that we were pleased for a period of time.

So far Aristotle has given us further reasons for thinking that pleasure is not a process. This has not been an entirely negative enterprise and indeed we have some positive results. Firstly, that pleasure is complete at any point of its duration; and secondly, that pleasure is indivisible or is some kind of whole. These are the characteristics that distinguish pleasure from processes. But we still do not have a positive account of pleasure. Aristotle is alleged to present one in the following passage:

> Every perceptual capacity is active in relation to its perceptible object and completely active when it is in good condition in relation to the finest of its perceptible objects. For this above all seems to be the character of complete activity, whether it is ascribed to the capacity or to the subject that has it. Hence for each capacity the best activity is the activity of the subject in the best condition in relation to the best object of the capacity.
>
> This activity will also be the most complete and the most pleasant. For every perceptual capacity and every sort of thought and study has its pleasure; the most pleasant activity is the most complete; and *the most complete is the activity of the subject in good condition in relation to the most excellent object of that capacity. Pleasure completes the activity.* (1174b15–24; emphasis added)

Aspects of this passage are obscure. It is clear, though, that Aristotle presents in it an analysis of the 'most complete activity'. The activity of any perceptual capacity is most complete when (a) it is in a good condition, by which Aristotle means that it is functionally operative, and (b) it is active with regard to its finest (*kalon*) object. Condition (a) seems relatively straightforward: a damaged perceptual capacity will not carry out its characteristic activity completely. Condition (b) presents problems. Just what is the finest object of a perceptual capacity? The word *kalon* is sometimes translated as 'beautiful' (a translation that underpins some English words like '*calli*graphy': beautiful writing) and so it's possible that Aristotle's thought is just that a perceptual capacity is only complete when it is engaged with the most beautiful of its objects. This might be interpreted as meaning that the exercise of our perceptual capacities is only complete when they are active with regard to the most 'aesthetically pleasing' objects. But I see no good reason to attribute such a view to Aristotle. It strikes me as far more likely that Aristotle means that the object of activity is most *excellent*, as Irwin translates '*kalon*' in the emphasized text. On this account, an activity is most complete if the perceptual capacity is active with regard to the most excellent object appropriate to it. This leaves mysterious quite what the most excellent objects are, but does not carry the unnecessarily restrictive implication that only aesthetically pleasing objects may complete activities.

Putting these problems to one side, for the moment, we can notice two further remarks: (i) the most complete activity is the most pleasant; and (ii) pleasure completes the activity. On the face of it, we still don't yet have an analysis of pleasure. We've been told what kind of activities are most pleasant (the most complete ones); and we've been told what makes those activities complete (pleasure). We have not been presented with an analysis of pleasure itself. This interpretative issue has led some commentators to reconsider Aristotle's principal objective in *NE* X.1–5. Is it to give a constitutive account of pleasure (that is, to say what pleasure is)? Or is it to give a functional account of pleasure (that is, to say what pleasure does)? There are compelling reasons for thinking Aristotle's primary objective is to specify the function (*ergon*) of pleasure: the most salient of which is the absence of an explicit analysis of pleasure itself. We've been told, for example, that pleasure completes an activity as a sort of consequent end (what pleasure does) (1174b34). Again, we've been told that 'pleasure increases [or stimulates] the activity' (what pleasure does) (1175b1). We have not been told what pleasure itself is.

If we accept such an interpretation there are at least two residual issues. Firstly, what is the function (*ergon*) of pleasure? Secondly, what are we to make of Aristotle's remarks at 1154b33–4 and at 1174a13, both of which suggest that his goal is to analyse pleasure? With regard to the first issue, Michael Pakaluk argues very persuasively that the *ergon* of pleasure is to 'bring activities to completion' (2004, p. 311).[52] His thought is that pleasure is a goal distinct from the activity, but the pursuit of that goal brings the activity to completion; that is, in aiming for pleasure the activity we perform meets conditions (a) and (b) above (ibid.). So the function of pleasure is that in our pursuit of it our activities are rendered complete. This is why it is important to bring our children up correctly with regard to pleasure and pain: through pursuing what is actually pleasant they will act virtuously.

But what then of Aristotle's claims to have presented analyses? We might be tempted to think the first of these at 1154b33–4 is an editorial insertion. As we have remarked above, the divisions of the *NE* we have today are unlikely to have been Aristotle's and the tidying up of the manuscript may well have included some comments Aristotle himself may not have endorsed. But this is not satisfactory. Presumably Aristotle thought he had indicated something about the nature of pleasure: it is something whole and indivisible; and it is the vitality of action (in Kant's memorable phrase 'pleasure is the feeling of life' (1790 [1952], p. 42). Certainly later thinkers treated pleasure as a basic concept that could not be further analysed (see, for example, Burke, p. 30).

We have, then, considered Aristotle's positive account of pleasure and have seen that a functional interpretation seems to sit better with the text.

X.5

Aristotle raises many interesting issues in this discussion. We'll concentrate on two points. First, Aristotle claims that pleasures vary with the activities they complete (1175a22–5). As Urmson (1988) put it, the pleasure of reading poetry is different from the pleasure of stamp collecting (p. 104). The second point follows from the first: pleasure has no value in itself. The value a pleasure has is determined by the value of the activity it is consequent upon (1175b25–35). Here, then, is Aristotle's response to the problem of the so-called despicable pleasures we considered above. Pleasure itself is neither praiseworthy nor deplorable. What we may call a despicable pleasure is the pleasure a person takes in a deplorable activity. So, if it is deplorable to eat one's children and I take pleasure in eating my children, then my pleasure is despicable.

Before we move to Aristotle's second discussion of *eudaimonia* it is worth drawing together the strands of the second discussion of pleasure. We have interpreted Aristotle as primarily concerned to identify the role of pleasure. The role of pleasure is to bring activities to completeness: that is, to be active with regard to the most excellent objects proper to our active faculties when those faculties are in full-functioning order and are unimpeded by defect. Pleasure itself is not identical to such activity, but is consequent upon it and as such varies with the activities it is consequent upon. Pleasure is neither good nor bad in itself: the apparent value of a pleasure is really the value of the activity it completes.

X.6

In *NE* X.6–8 Aristotle discusses the nature of *eudaimonia*. This is, in itself, unsurprising: we were told at 1098a22–3 that the sketch of *eudaimonia* articulated in *NE* I.7 would be filled in later. What is surprising is that the second discussion of *eudaimonia* appears to be at odds both with theses elsewhere in the *NE* and, indeed, with our intuitions about the good life. This presents us with a difficulty: either to explain away the apparent conflict between the two accounts or to explain the presence of a conflicting account in the *NE* as we have it. We will examine these issues below. However, I think it's worth reminding ourselves that we are consulting Aristotle's text with a view to the light it sheds on a question that has significance for each of us. This is not to say that we should simply dismiss the text where we find apparent contradictions: the following discussion, I hope, indicates the seriousness of the issue. Rather, it is to say that we should examine the texts with a view to clarifying our own opinions about the nature of the best life for humankind.

It is clear that in these chapters Aristotle intends to contrast different kinds of lives. The precise nature of those lives, and their correspondence to the 'lives' of *NE* I.5, is more controversial. In Chapter 6 Aristotle recalls the conceptual constraints from *NE* I.7: the *eudaimon* life is complete and is self-sufficient (1176b3–7; cf. 1097a27–b21). He then notes that the 'life of amusement' appears to satisfy these constraints and is a contender for the title '*eudaimonia*'. We seem to choose amusements or pastimes for their own sakes and not for the sake of anything else: hence they are complete and if an activity is complete it follows that it is self-sufficient (1097b8). This life is sometimes thought to reprise the 'life of pleasure' that is so tersely dismissed at 1095b19–21. However, in this commentary at least, we have taken Aristotle at his word and have interpreted the 'life of pleasure' as a life of carnal gratification, the rational part of which is absent (cf. 1098a2; 1147b4). It is not clear that Aristotle has in mind so restricted a life here (though cf. 1176b10–13 and 1176b21–2) and we can presumably include pastimes in which the activity of the rational part of the soul is present.

What is clear is that Aristotle doesn't think the life of amusement is the *eudaimon* life (1176b29). This is because even if amusements are complete, they are certainly not the *most* complete end of life: 'it would be absurd if the end [of human life] were amusement and all our lifelong efforts and sufferings aimed at amusing ourselves' (1176b29–31). This is, I think, true and surely the character of the lives of some of those people who attempt to live a 'life of amusement' demonstrates this.[53] Furthermore, it is not even clear that the activity of amusement is itself complete. We amuse ourselves, Aristotle claims, to relax and we desire relaxation so that we may undertake other actions (1176b35–6). This may well be true, but we shouldn't press the point too far. It is not obviously true, for example, that a person must consciously conceive of relaxation as preparation for a further activity when he listens to a record.

X.7–8

So far, then, Aristotle has dismissed the 'life of amusement' as an analysis of the *eudaimon* life. He now introduces two further 'lives' and appears to judge their respective claims to the accolade *eudaimon*. These chapters are a matter of intense controversy for in them Aristotle seems to judge that a *eudaimon* life is a 'life of contemplation',[54] and that a life lived in accordance with the other virtues is in some way 'secondary'. This apparent judgement is a source of disquiet for (at least) two reasons: (1) it presents us with an interpretative difficulty concerning the relationship of the two passages (Aristotle appears to have one view of *eudaimonia* in *NE* I and another in *NE* X); and (2) it conflicts with some of our intuitions about the best life, both in terms of what strikes us as attractive and in terms of what strikes us as 'moral'. We will begin by characterizing the two 'lives', thereby exposing issues (1) and (2). We will then consider some possible responses.

In Chapter 7 Aristotle claims that: 'complete *eudaimonia* will be [an] activity in accord with its proper virtue; and we have said that this activity is the activity of contemplation' (1177a17–18). This certainly seems to be an explicit statement about the nature of *eudaimonia*: it is the activity of contemplation. The activity of contemplation is taken to be the possession of, and reflection on, knowledge. Since knowledge is only of what is necessary (1139b21), it follows that contemplation is the reflection on necessary truths about the world. Aristotle goes on to provide us with six reasons for thinking that the activity of contemplation is the supreme activity for human beings:

(i)   Understanding (*nous*) is the supreme element of the human and its objects are the supreme objects of knowledge.
(ii) Contemplation is the most continuous activity humans are capable of and *eudaimonia* is something continuous (permanent or stable) (cf. 1105a35).
(iii) Activity in accordance with wisdom is supremely pleasant and *eudaimonia* is thought to be whatever is supremely pleasant (cf. 1099a25).

(iv) Contemplation is (the most) self-sufficient and *eudaimonia* is self-sufficient (cf. 1097b8–16).

(v) Contemplation is the only activity performed just for its own sake (cf. 1097a25–b6).

(vi) *Eudaimonia* depends on leisure (freedom) but the exercise of the virtues (other than contemplation) denies us leisure.

The general strategy, then, is to recall the characteristics of *eudaimonia* established elsewhere in the *NE* and then to argue that contemplation has all those characteristics (or has them to a greater extent than any other activity). He further argues for the supremacy of the activity of understanding in *NE* X.8 at 1178b9–24. There Aristotle reasons from the claims (a) that the gods are (assumed to be) the most supremely *eudaimon* beings and (b) that the gods exclusively contemplate to the conclusion (c) that the activity of contemplation is the supreme activity.[55] So, the 'life of contemplation' is godlike and we are only capable of it because of what is divine in us.

In *NE* X.8 Aristotle introduces the 'life of virtue concerned with action' and states that this is a *eudaimon* life in a 'secondary way' (1178a9–10). Since he immediately refers to 'just and brave actions', we may fairly assume that he has in mind here a life throughout which a person exercises the virtues of character as expounded in *NE* III.6–IV. He recalls that virtue of character is properly concerned with feelings (cf. 1105b27) and that virtue of character is inseparable from practical wisdom (cf. 1144b31–2). Since these virtues are concerned with feeling they belong to the compound of the part of the soul with reason and the part of the soul obedient to it.

This is the 'life' the *NE* seems to have been impressing on us as *eudaimon* throughout the text: five books (II–VI) have been dedicated to an examination of these virtues and the remaining three (VII–IX) are situated in the context of those virtues. But we are now told that this life of virtue is dependent to a far greater extent on external goods than the life of contemplation. For although both lives require sustenance and some measure of external goods, actions expressive of generosity require wealth and actions expressive of temperance require the resources for intemperance and so on (117825ff.). The activity of contemplation, however, requires none of these (in itself) and so is more self-sufficient. The overwhelmingly apparent implication is that the life of contemplation is superior to the life of virtue in action.

Having briefly sketched the two 'lives' Aristotle wants to compare, we can now see the force of problems (1) and (2) that were introduced above. Problem (1), recall, was about the interpretation of the *NE* as a coherent philosophical treatise. We noted the dispute between those who interpret the *NE* inclusively and those who interpret it dominantly. The claim that *eudaimonia* is self-sufficient, i.e. lacking in nothing, seemed to suggest that it was a complex good comprising the activity of all the virtues referred to in *NE* II.7. This suggested that an inclusivist interpretation of *eudaimonia* was correct. But the remarks of *NE* X.7–8 appear to suggest that this interpretation is wrong and that the *single* activity of contemplation is constitutive of *eudaimonia*, which suggests that a dominant interpretation is correct. What are we to say of this apparent contradiction? Does the second account simply supersede the first account? Are the 'lives' exclusive of one another? Are the accounts actually, though not apparently, consistent with one another?

Problem (2) was that the 'life of contemplation' appeared to conflict with some of our intuitions about the nature of the best life for human beings. I will restrict my comments to just two issues here. The first is that it is far from obvious that a 'life of contemplation' will appeal to many human beings. The suggestion that we should strive to contemplate necessary truths about nature for as long as we can bear throughout our short little lives must, to any ear, sound highly implausible. Surely, it will be insisted, a decent human life will include a range of different activities. While Aristotle appears to allow this (see, for example, 1176b32–1177a2), he clearly emphasizes that we are only *eudaimon* to the extent that we contemplate (1178b25–33). The second issue concerns our intuitions about the moral acceptability of the 'life of contemplation'. The concern is this. If the source of value in life is the activity of contemplation, then it seems I should only engage in some activity if it ultimately promotes my activity of contemplation. It seems rational, then, for me to cease to engage in activities that conflict with my contemplation. So if, for example, I come to recognize that having a family is detracting from, rather than promoting, my contemplation, it is reasonable for me to leave my family (cf. Cooper 1975, p. 98). But surely, it is thought, my leaving my family to contemplate necessary truths is deeply immoral and I shouldn't do it. Apparently, Aristotle is recommending something which conflicts with our intuitions about the living of decent lives.

Having fleshed out the problems, we must now examine potential responses to them. I will start with problem (1). We should note that some commentators are of the view that *NE* X.6–8 did not originally belong in the *NE* at all (see, for example, Annas 1993, p. 214) and so the matter of explaining the relationship between that passage and the rest of the text is irrelevant. Although I won't consider it further, there are some reasons to support this view. For example, the criterion of 'self-sufficiency' specified at 1177a27–b2 has a different sense from the criterion of 'self-sufficiency' at 1097b14–16. In the former passage self-sufficiency refers to what can be done without external aid, whereas in the latter passage it refers to what makes life desirable and lacking in nothing. In itself this is not necessarily problematic: what is problematic is Aristotle's apparent attempt to justify his analysis of *eudaimonia* as contemplation on the basis that it meets the original criteria specified in *NE* I.7. Nor will I consider some more extreme responses that include the astonishing claim that Aristotle was, in *NE* X.7–8, being ironic (Molin 1983).

So, assuming *NE* X.6–8 to be a sincere and genuine constituent of the treatise as Aristotle intended, what are we to say about the apparent conflict between *NE* I and X over the nature of *eudaimonia*?[56] To begin with, we should recall our earlier account of *eudaimonia*. I suggested that a *eudaimon* life is a life shaped and directed by the exercise of virtue. Following Cooper's terminology, we referred to *eudaimonia* so construed as a second-order good. It is a good that is not identified with any one particular first-order good, but is rather the good of having a life of first-order goods ordered such that their true value and significance is embodied in their proper place in that life. The account of *eudaimonia* in *NE* X identifies it with contemplation (*theoria*), which is the activity of understanding (*nous*). It is very tempting indeed to see this as a first-order good: that is, an activity on a par with doing the washing-up, making a gift and helping one's son tie his shoelaces. So interpreted, Aristotle seems to be suggesting in *NE* X that we should try to maximize one of our first-order goods, contemplating necessary truths. However, a *eudaimon* life (i.e. a life *throughout which* one performs actions constitutive of *eudaimonia*) is then, strictly speaking, impossible because, as Aristotle readily admits, one cannot continuously contemplate. Nonetheless, he claims we should strive to contemplate as much as possible throughout our lives. We have, then, an interpretation of *NE* I.7 that suggests *eudaimonia* comprises a range of goods appropriately ordered and an interpretation of *NE* X.7–8 that suggests *eudaimonia* is the single activity of contemplation maximized as far as is humanly possible.

It strikes me as immensely significant, in this context, that Aristotle reminds us that 'what is proper to each thing's nature is supremely best and most pleasant for it' (1178a6–7). Since the nature of the human being is composite (something clearly not denied in these chapters), he cannot be recommending that we live preternaturally. This is clearly acknowledged at 1178b5–8: 'insofar as he [the *eudaimon*] is a human being, however, and lives together with a number of other human beings, he chooses to do the actions that accord with virtue'. And since these actions 'accord with virtue' it cannot but be the case that they imply the active presence of practical wisdom (1178a17ff.). It follows, then, that the shape of the *eudaimon*'s life will include the ordering of various activities according to their true value and significance. At no point, to my mind, does Aristotle recommend our rejecting our true nature to try (in vain) to become what we are not.

But the point in the preceding paragraph seems to be at odds with Aristotle's rejection of the proverbs 'Think human, since you are human' and 'Think mortal, since you are mortal' and with his insistence that 'as far as we can, we ought to be pro-immortal and go to all lengths to live a life in accord with our supreme element' (1177b33–1178a1). Surely this directly contradicts my claim that to the extent that Aristotle conceives of our nature as composite, he cannot be recommending we try to become *super*human. The aspirational tenor of the passage cannot be denied: but what exactly is being extolled? To see this, we must consider further the nature of contemplation.

Understanding (*nous*) is explicitly identified as our supreme element (1177a20) and contemplation is the activity of understanding. It is worth pausing to consider the sense of the Greek word, *theoria*. This literally means '(intellectual) seeing', 'observing' or 'attending to'. The interpretation of *theoria* as a first-order good equivalent to the contemplation of knowledge (i.e. necessary truths) is based on arguments (i) and (iii) above. Although elsewhere in the *NE nous* is assigned a role in the exercise of practical wisdom (1143a33–b10), commentators assume that this role is included in the 'secondary' life of virtue in action in *NE* X.8. So the apparent conflict between *NE* I and X depends on narrowly interpreting *theoria* as the contemplation of necessary truths.

However, the sense attributed to *nous* in *NE* X.7 suggests that the interpretation in the previous paragraph is not quite right. For there Aristotle consistently identifies it with the 'ruling' or 'controlling' part of the soul (1177a15; 1178a3–4). To interpret *nous* along these lines seems to me quite consistent with the activity constitutive of *eudaimonia* in *NE* I. It is that activity of grasping what is, all things considered, the best action to perform and, in its theoretical deployment, it grasps the most basic truths of a discipline. Furthermore, Aristotle has argued in *NE* IX.9 that in perceiving or understanding, we contemplate our perception or understanding. It seems reasonable, then, that Aristotle could have in mind our contemplation of the entire activity of *nous* in both its practical and theoretical deployments. There is no pretending that this resolves all the problems of the text, but it strikes me as a possible and harmonious resolution of the alleged conflict.

What, though, are we to say of Aristotle's clear statement that a life of virtue in action is 'secondary' to a life of contemplation? Indeed, on the interpretation sketched above, how could there be any distinction between them if the activity of *nous* is present in both? One thought is that the 'secondary' life described in *NE* X.8 excludes the contemplation of necessary truths and only includes the ceaseless exercise of justice, generosity and bravery. This would suggest that the best kind of life is the one in which the two are combined, and that to dedicate oneself to the exercise of virtue in action is to miss out on one crucial constituent of the *eudaimon* life. Aristotle's comment that the virtue of understanding is something apart from this (1178a23) might be thought to support this. But all it can really lay claim to is the idea that understanding is separable from the activity of practical wisdom and virtue of character.

I will close with a brief remark about problem (2). This was, you will recall, the problem that the life of contemplation interpreted as the maximization of attending to necessary truths to the detriment of our life with others is immoral. I think it clear, from the sketch above, that this is not a serious problem for the interpretation we have developed. For Aristotle is not, on this interpretation, committed to the idea that the *eudaimon* person should subordinate everything to the maximization of contemplation. He lives a human life and with other humans, and to that extent he will practise the virtues of character. However, consistently with that he will be active in his attendance to the truths about the nature of the world and in that he will be fascinated by the peculiarity of the human condition and circumstance.

Study questions

1. Are the discussions of pleasure in the *NE* consistent with one another?
2. Does Aristotle succeed in refuting Eudoxus' position?
3. What is pleasure according to Aristotle?
4. What is a life of contemplation?
5. Does Aristotle have a consistent account of *eudaimonia*?

CHAPTER 4

RECEPTION AND INFLUENCE

INTRODUCTION

In this section we will examine aspects of the legacy of the *NE*. I use the word 'aspects' advisedly for the account that follows does not pretend to (anything approaching) completeness. The *NE* has a defining place in the development of our efforts to understand ourselves and our relationships to others. The truth of this is disclosed by the number of its ideas that strike new readers as platitudinous. There is good reason for any apparent lack of novelty.

The *NE*'s influence stretches from the work of Theophrastus, Aristotle's successor as the head of the Lyceum, who published *Characters*, in which he expatiates upon vicious traits of character, to Philippa Foot's most recent volume *Natural Goodness*, which develops the idea that vice is a natural defect. To chart the history of the *NE* comprehensively is not our purpose; in fact, our discussion will only pick up on the influence of the *NE* on a very few subsequent philosophers and writers.

We will begin by commenting on the use made of the *NE* by Saint Thomas Aquinas and what is today referred to as 'natural law' theory. We will then address the relationship between the *NE* and Mill's *Utilitarianism* (1861). Finally, we will turn to the twentieth century and the 'revival', as it is sometimes known, of virtue (or aretaic) ethics. This revival has its origins in Elizabeth Anscombe's famous paper 'Modern Moral Philosophy' (1958). Subsequent philosophers took themselves as addressing the 'three theses' Anscombe argues for in her paper and we will briefly consider some of their philosophy.

I AQUINAS

Saint Thomas Aquinas was a Dominican friar engaged in, *inter alia*, Aristotelian exegesis in the thirteenth century. The purpose of his interpretation of Aristotle, and of his research in general, was the reconciliation of the Church and philosophy. At that time, the work of Aristotle was deemed a threat to the Church. In his exposition of Aristotle's philosophy, Aquinas rejected some of the controversial Aristotelian theses and made his work acceptable to the Church. So acceptable, in fact, that the subsequent association of Aristotle's writing and the Church provoked hostility. Hobbes, writing in the seventeenth century, declared that the Reformation owed much to 'the bringing of the Philosophy and Doctrine of *Aristotle* into religion by the school-men' (*Leviathan* 1.12). (Incidentally, Hobbes's inimical attitude went deeper: in the chapter entitled 'Of the DARK-NESSSE from VAIN PHILOSOPHY' he declares that 'I beleeve that scare anything can be more absurdly said in naturall Philosophy than that which is now called *Aristotles Metaphysiques* . . . nor more ignorantly, than a great part of his *Ethiques*' (*Leviathan* 4.46).)

Aquinas prepared a very detailed commentary on the *NE*, which remains tremendously useful today. However, he most fully deployed his grasp of Aristotle's thought in *Summa Theologiae* (the 'Summation of Theology'). Consider the following examples from Aquinas' discussion of virtue:

> By the word virtue we mean a certain excellence of perfection of potential. Now we measure anything's perfection primarily in its relation to its goal and the goal of potential is realising it. So a potential is called perfect when it is set to be actualised. (1a.2ae.55)

> Drunkenness and unrestrained drinking are bad because they lack reason's order. But what lacks reason may require perfection from some lesser power in its own realm, even though that conflicts with or detracts from reason. But perfection of such power, when it involves lack of reason, can't be called virtue. (1a.2ae.55)

These two short passages are clearly Aristotelian. In the first, Aquinas claims that virtue is what makes something perfect relative to its goal (cf. 1106a17–24). In the second passage we are told that a capability or power that is not directed or shaped by reason cannot be called a virtue (cf. 1144b16–17). It might seem, then, that Aquinas adopted Aristotle's position wholesale. But to assert this would be a mistake. Despite his endorsement of many of Aristotle's claims and theses, Aquinas argued for his own distinctive conclusions. For example, Aquinas thought that the goal of a human life was God, conceived of as personified goodness.

Aquinas is associated with 'natural law' theory because of passages such as this: a law is 'a kind of rational ordering for the common good, promulgated by the one who takes care of the community' (1a.11ae.90.4c). However, it's not clear that Aquinas himself would have endorsed the later use made of the notion of a 'natural law'. In its later application we find the derivation of laws which, if observed, cause the life of the agent to be good. The laws isolate what is good for human beings based on their function. So, for example, the function of copulation is described as the 'progeneration of the species'. The copulative activity of human beings is, then, good only to the extent that it achieves its goal, *viz* the issuing of offspring.

Many people, regardless of any religious inclinations, do not find this view acceptable, presumably on the ground that it's not clear that the function of copulative activity is the progeneration of the species. Perhaps the function of copulation is something else, such as 'the promotion and development of bonds of love between persons'. Human copulation would, then, be good or excellent to the extent that persons engaged in it developed such loving bonds between them.

II MILL

John Stuart Mill argued for the 'Greatest Happiness Principle' in his *Utilitarianism* (1861). There are, at first glance, several striking parallels between Mill's work and Aristotle's. Mill presents his inquiry as a search for the supreme good: 'from the dawn of philosophy, the question concerning the *summum bonum*, or, what is the same thing, concerning the foundation of morality, has been accounted the main problem in speculative thought' (p. 131; cf. 1094a1–b11). Mill also deploys principles that are redolent of Aristotle's: 'Of two pleasures, if there be one to which all or almost all who have experienced both give a preference, irrespective of any feeling or moral obligation to prefer it, that is the more desirable' (p. 139; cf. 1173a2–3). And thirdly, Mill identifies as the 'ultimate end' of human life the achievement of *happiness* (p. 137).

However, despite these superficial parallels there are deep differences between the two philosophers. Setting the curious remark at 1177b3–4 aside, Aristotle is not a utilitarian. For Aristotle, the state of the agent expressed in his action is decisive in our assessment of the value of that action. And as we have noted in our discussion of *NE* II.4, two people could perform similar actions that nonetheless express two different states of character. For Aristotle only the person who expresses a virtuous state of his character in his action is to be accorded the highest commendation. For Mill, however, the state of character is irrelevant in our assessment of the value of an action. He thinks that 'actions are right in proportion as they tend to promote happiness, wrong as they intend to produce the reverse of happiness (p. 137). It is the value of the *consequences* of an action that determine its moral value. Now, of course, Mill thinks there are estimable dispositions of a person's character (p. 150). But the value of these dispositions depends on the value of the actions they issue in. So, we have an asymmetry here between the two views: Aristotle thinks that the value of actions depends on the value of the states of character from which they flow; Mill thinks the value of dispositions of character depends on the value of the actions they tend to produce.

A further point of disagreement is over the constitution of the *summum bonum*. As we have seen Aristotle identifies this with a certain kind of life throughout which a person exercises the virtues of the rational part of the soul. Mill conceives of the *summum bonum* as happiness, which he identifies with pleasure. At first sight, our contemporary conception of happiness is closer to Mill's than to Aristotle's because people tend to think of happiness as a psychological state. Furthermore, Mill's account of pleasure is more subtle than Bentham's, who devised what he referred to as the felicific calculus, which attempted to quantify pleasure (something necessary if one is to compare the pleasure of two courses of action). Mill, however, recognized qualitative differences in pleasures too (cf. 1176b18–24). Despite Mill's distinction between higher and lower pleasures (pp. 137ff.), Aristotle would reject Mill's overall account. As we have seen, Aristotle doesn't think pleasure is valuable in itself: its value is determined by the value of the activity it is consequent upon. So although Mill's utilitarianism may have been influenced by the concepts of the *NE* it diverges from Aristotle's usage.

III ANSCOMBE

There are three explicit theses of Anscombe's 'Modern Moral Philosophy': (i) that we should desist from moral philosophy until we have an adequate moral psychology; (ii) that we should, if possible, jettison the concepts of '*moral* obligation' and '*moral* duty' from our vocabulary because they belong to an earlier, now defunct, conception of ethics; and (iii) that differences between the British moral philosophers from the nineteenth century onwards are of little importance (p. 26). Putting (iii) to one side, we can concentrate on the relationship between (ii) and (i). Anscombe thinks that we should reject the law conception of ethics, upon which the concepts of 'moral obligation' and 'moral duty' depend, and return to an ethics based on virtue. But since, according to Anscombe, we don't have a very precise conception of the relevant psychological concepts, for example 'pleasure' and 'action', we should cease to do moral philosophy until we have clarified those concepts.

Let's consider, very briefly, Anscombe's argument for (ii). She thinks that the concepts 'ought' and 'should' have perfectly ordinary everyday senses. We may say that an engine *should* be oiled, for example, because otherwise it will run badly (p. 30). However, she notes that the concepts in their moral application have acquired a 'special sense' that connotes a juridical obligation of a person to act in a certain way. Consider the claims that 'You shouldn't exceed 70 mph on the motorway' and 'You shouldn't lie to your partner'. The first expresses a law as formulated by human beings; the second expresses a 'moral law'. The notion of a moral law emerges historically from the Church, which endorses the claim that a supernatural being, God, prescribes laws governing human conduct. Since, however, we have resigned the belief in a divine lawgiver our concepts of 'moral obligation' and 'moral duty' have lost their root (p. 31). The word 'obligation', for example, retains 'the suggestion of force and [is] apt to have a strong psychological effect, but [it] no longer signifies a real concept at all' (p. 33).

So, if we accept that the concept of 'moral obligation' implies a law conception of ethics, and if we accept that we have rejected the basis for such a conception of ethics, then we can admit that certain of our concepts no longer make sense. We should cease to use expressions like 'Stealing is wrong' and replace them with expressions like 'Stealing is unjust'. It would be a 'great improvement if instead of "morally wrong" one always named a genus, such as untruthful, unchaste, unjust. We should no longer ask whether something was "wrong", passing directly from some description of an action to this notion; we should ask whether it was unjust' (p. 34). But, Anscombe contends, we need an account of justice and injustice, i.e. an account of virtue. This is a point that, according to Anscombe, Aristotle failed to make clear (p. 30). The baselessness of our current moral terms requires us to return to terms that express virtuous states of character. But we don't well understand virtuous states of character and so we need to clarify our moral psychology to account for them.

IV CONTEMPORARY VIRTUE ETHICS

The renewed interest in the virtues has its origins in Anscombe's paper. It's true that there were philosophers working on the virtues before Anscombe's paper, but the approach taken since has as its starting point Anscombe's recommendations. In their introduction to *Oxford Readings in Virtue Ethics*, Crisp and Slote remark that few philosophers have addressed thesis (i) of Anscombe's paper (p. 2). A notable exception to this is N. J. H. Dent's *The Moral Psychology of the Virtues* (1984). Dent's starting point is Anscombe's comment that we don't well understand the nature of virtues and vices. In his view the insights of Plato and Aristotle have been obscured in subsequent philosophy and he intends to recover them (p. 2). His text is not, however, an exercise in Platonic and Aristotelian exegesis: Dent presents his own arguments for the conception of the desiring elements of the soul he believes we find in their writing. In the course of the book the concepts associated with virtuous action, for example, 'practical reason', 'desire', 'deliberation', etc., are clarified to great effect. In particular, he presents a very cogent case for thinking that (some) desires are based on the exercise of practical reason. That is to say, the presence or absence of a certain desire in a person owes not to the blessings (or curses) of nature, but is dependent upon the person's estimation of the importance of objects in their environment.

Among the philosophers who have addressed Anscombe's thesis (ii) is Alisdair MacIntyre. He argues in *After Virtue* (1981 [1985]) that contemporary morality is in a state of crisis because of what he takes to be the rejection of Aristotle's thought in seventeenth-century Europe (p. 37; p. 56). He contends that in the rejection of Aristotle's thought, the concepts of *ergon* and of there being an ultimate human *telos* were rejected too. Thus eighteenth-century moral philosophy inherited a set of moral injunctions divorced from the conceptual scheme in terms of which they made sense. They then faced the (impossible) task of trying to find an alternative basis for their moral inheritance on reason or passion (p. 55). MacIntyre contends that these philosophers failed. Having accounted for this crisis, he recommends that we revive the concept of a virtue. His own account of the virtues is situated in terms of what he calls 'practices'. A practice is some 'established co-operative human activity through which goods internal to that form of activity are realised in the course of trying to achieve those standards of excellence which are appropriate to . . . that form of activity' (p. 187). So, playing bridge is a practice if we play for goods internal to the game but not if we play for some external good, such as winning the esteem of a suitor. MacIntyre then examines the role of virtue in (a) the activities of an individual's life, (b) the activities in the context of an individual's whole life and (c) the relation of the individual's life to that of his community. Although his account has stimulated considerable discussion, it must be noted that his interpretation of some writers has been questioned.

I will conclude this brief characterization of recent work by mentioning Rosalind Hursthouse's *On Virtue Ethics* (1999). Hursthouse is a neo-Aristotelian and directly addresses the main objections to ethical theories based on virtue, as a serious alternative to consequentialist and deontological ethical theories. (It should be noted that Hursthouse herself is not minded to reinforce the apparent divisions between these approaches with a view to defending virtue ethics as distinctive.) Of particular interest is her examination of Aristotle and Kant on the motivation for virtuous action. Her discussion of 'acting for the sake of the fine' and 'acting for the sake of duty' brings the work of these writers closer than they are traditionally presented as being. I would recommend those readers interested in examining the use that can be made of Aristotelian ideas in the discussions of ethical theory to consult her volume.

CONCLUSION

We have in this section taken a very selective look at some of the writing that has its ultimate source in the *NE*. This should, I believe, be taken as a testament to its power to illuminate the nature of the active life of human beings. In it we find, I believe, the most insightful and comprehensive assessment of the nature of the best life for human beings and to that extent it merits our continued study. Whether or not we endorse Aristotle's solutions to the problems he sets himself, we cannot ignore his questions.

NOTES

1 The following brief examination of method should be supplemented. A good place to start is Bostock, pp. 214–35 and Barnes (1980), though readers should note the latter presumes some Greek. I am indebted to both texts.

2 Cf. John Rawls' use of 'reflective equilibrium' in his *A Theory of Justice* (1971) for a contemporary application of a very Aristotelian method.

3 Cf. Stuart Hampshire's comparison of Aristotle and Spinoza on this point: '[Spinoza] had not followed Aristotle in accepting the actual limits of human knowledge as they were in his time', p. 57.

4 My citation of this text should not be taken as implying that the object of the science of happiness and the object of Aristotle's inquiry are identical.

5 I owe this analogy to Kenny (1966).

6 For a good discussion of these issues see Kraut (1979).

7 Aristotle himself doesn't seem to think it possible for a person to be virtuous without doing what is virtuous (1105b13–15). He perhaps here is concerned merely with the popular account or of cases in which a person who, having acquired virtue, suffers misfortune (cf. *NE* I.10–11).

8 Bostock gives a longer discussion, pp. 29–31, and there are useful notes in Broadie (Rowe and Broadie 2002) and Irwin (1985 [1999]). Fine (1993) presents a full-length discussion of the matter.

9 Aristotle's full theory of the soul is contained in *De Anima*.

10 Essential reading here is Ackrill (1974).

11 See Irwin (1999) in Sherman (ed.) (1999) for discussion of these issues.

12 Curiously, though, Aristotle omits all reference to pleasure and pain in what is generally regarded as his definition of virtue at 1107a1–3. However, the corresponding passage in the *EE* explicitly incorporates pleasure and pain into the definition: 'moral excellence is a mean relative to each individual himself and is concerned with certain means in pleasure and pain, in the pleasant and painful' (1222a10–12).

13 I have benefited from Hursthouse (1999). See her discussion, pp. 121–40.

14 There is an interesting exchange between Williams and Hursthouse about the interpretation of (ii) in their contributions to *Aristotle and Moral Realism* (ed. Heineman).

15 There has been an interesting debate about (iii) in recent discussions about the very existence of character traits. See, for example, Harman (1999) and Athanassoulis (2001). Harman's point is, I think, wide of the mark.
16 These negative arguments are to be found in Bostock, pp. 36–7.
17 An excellent discussion of this chapter can be found in Curzer (1996).
18 Hughes, p. 119.
19 Bostock, p. 105.
20 Hughes, pp. 120–3.
21 Ross translates *prohairesis* 'choice' and Crisp 'rational choice'.
22 Urmson characterizes this in the modern idiom of intensional and extensional objects. The intensional object is the good; the extensional object is the apparent good (1988), pp. 57–9.
23 See, for example, Urmson (1988), pp. 59–61 and Hughes (pp. 137–43) for accessible discussions.
24 See Goldie for a good assessment of indirect proofs such as Aristotle's.
25 Most translations use either one of these terms. Schopenhauer notes that the scope of courage is wider than that of bravery: the latter applying to courage on the battlefield (1970), p. 135. Urmson thinks that 'valour' would better reflect what Aristotle has in mind, though he too uses 'bravery' (1988), p. 63.
26 For brief introductions to all the virtues Aristotle discusses see Broadie (2002), pp. 23–37.
27 I would recommend in this respect Theophrastus' *Characters*.
28 For a discussion of the 'fine' see my comments on p. 41.
29 Cf. the states that resemble bravery in *NE* III.6–9.
30 The nature of this characteristic is developed and explored in Veblen (1899), especially in Chapters 3 and 4.
31 A perceptive and balanced examination of these matters can be found in Curzer (1991).
32 See Curzer (1991) for further exposition of these points.
33 On moral development see Wollheim (1985), section VII.
34 I owe this reference to Urmson (1988), p. 71.
35 Although I haven't gone into it in the main text, the practice of holding doors open for others is quite complex. It involves quite subtle judgements about, for example, how far away a person has to be before holding the door open appears creepy or out of place.
36 Some desires, though, are not susceptible to the same extent, e.g. bodily desires (1118a25ff.).
37 Though cf. 1097b2–5.
38 This interpretation assumes that 'doing the right action *accidentally*' is not, at least in the sense specified in *NE* VI.2, strictly speaking an action at all.
39 I recommend the reader bear these comments in mind before approaching *NE* X.7.
40 See, for example, Cooper (1975), pp. 40–6, Kenny (1978), pp. 170–2 and, more recently, Bostock, pp. 89–93.
41 Matthews provides a thorough account of the variety of phenomena that might be grouped under the name 'weakness of will'.
42 See Broadie (1991), Bostock and Pakaluk (2005).

43 I owe this presentation of the problem of interpretation to Broadie (2002, pp. 385–7).

44 See Holton (2003) for a stimulating discussion.

45 For a different interpretation that renders Books VII and X coherent see Owen (1971–2).

46 Though cf. Annas (1977) who suggests that 'in an important way the course on friendship fails to fit into the *Ethics*. The obvious explanation is that it was written earlier, perhaps with [Plato's] *Lysis* specifically in mind, and was added later to the collection of discussions that make up the *Ethics*' (p. 554).

47 Cf. Kant, who astonishingly reduced marriage to an agreement between persons for the 'reciprocal use of each other's sexual organs' (1967, p. 235).

48 On this basis Cooper interprets Aristotle as referring to friendships not of perfect virtue, but of character. If this is correct most of us could hope for something more than 'mercenary people who form friendships for utility' (1158a22). Cooper's suggestion however is difficult to square with key passages (see, for example, *NE* XI.4).

49 I strongly recommend Peter Goldie's *On Personality* (2004) for its discussion both of character and of the differences between personality and character traits. See especially pp. 27–32.

50 Cf. Kant, *The Metaphysic of Morals*, p. 392.

51 If we conceive of pleasure as a state of the subject, can we make sense of the idea of a person being mistaken about his own state? If a person says he is experiencing pleasure, are there circumstances in which we're entitled to say that he's wrong?

52 Pakaluk's entire discussion is worth consulting on this matter.

53 Consider the fictional example of des Esseintes in Huysmans (1884 [1959]).

54 Irwin translates 'study'. I have followed Ross's translation here, but will discuss the Greek word '*theoria*' below.

55 The absurdity of the gods engaging in anything other than contemplation is illustrated by the curious occasion when God is represented as effectively apologizing to Amos regarding his treatment of Jacob (Amos 7:1–6). I owe this reference to R. Janis (pers. comm.).

56 I will not include here a survey of the responses commentators have made: readers interested in comparing these should consult Bostock, pp. 203–9.

GUIDE TO FURTHER READING

1. WORKS BY ARISTOTLE IN TRANSLATION

The Complete Works of Aristotle 2 vols. Ed. J. Barnes (Princeton: Princeton University Press, 1984)
Nicomachean Ethics trans. T. Irwin (Indianapolis: Hackett, 1985 [1999])
Nicomachean Ethics trans. W.D. Ross in *The Complete Works of Aristotle*
Nicomachean Ethics trans. C. Rowe with notes by S. Broadie (Oxford: Oxford University Press, 2002)
The Ethics of Aristotle trans. J.A.K. Thomson (London: Penguin, 1955)
Eudemian Ethics trans. J. Solomon in *The Complete Works of Aristotle*
Magna Moralia trans. St. G. Stock in *The Complete Works of Aristotle*
Virtues and Vices trans. J. Solomon in *The Complete Works of Aristotle*
Rhetoric trans. W. Rhys Roberts in *The Complete Works of Aristotle*

2. COMMENTARIES

Bostock, D. *Aristotle's Ethics* (Oxford: Oxford University Press, 2000)
Broadie, S. *Ethics with Aristotle* (New York: Oxford University Press, 1991)
Cooper, J. M. *Reason and the Human Good in Aristotle* (Indianapolis: Hackett, 1975)
Fine, G. *On Ideas* (Oxford: Clarendon Press, 1993)
Hardie, W.F.R. *Aristotle's Ethical Theory* (Oxford: Clarendon Press, 1968 [1980])
Hughes, G.J. *Aristotle on Ethics* (London: Routledge, 2001)
Hutchinson, D.S. *The Virtues of Aristotle* (London: Routledge, 1986)
Kenny, A. *The Aristotelian Ethics* (Oxford: Clarendon Press, 1978)
——*Aristotle's Theory of the Will* (New Haven: Yale University Press, 1979)
Joachim, H.H. *Aristotle, The Nicomachean Ethics* (Oxford: Oxford University Press, 1955)
Pakaluk, M. *Aristotle:* Nicomachean Ethics, *Books VIII and IX* (Oxford: Clarendon Press, 1980)
——*Aristotle's Nicomachean Ethics* (Cambridge: Cambridge University Press, 2005)

Price, A.W. *Love and Friendship in Plato and Aristotle* (New York: Oxford University Press, 1989)
Ross, W.D *Aristotle* (New York: Routledge, 1923 [1995])
Urmson, J.O. *Aristotle's Ethics* (Oxford: Blackwell, 1988)

3. COLLECTIONS OF ARTICLES

Barnes, J., Schofield, M., Sorabji, R. eds. *Articles on Aristotle*, vol. 2 (London: Duckworth, 1977)
Irwin, T.E. ed. *Classical Philosophy, vol. 5: Aristotle's Ethics* (New York: Garland Publishing, 1995)
Heinamen, R ed. *Aristotle and Moral Realism* (Boulder: Westview, 1995)
Rorty, A.O. ed. *Essays on Aristotle's Ethics* (Berkeley: University of California, 1980)
Sherman, N. ed. *Aristotle's Ethics: Critical Essays* (Lanham: Rowman & Littlefield, 1999)

4. ARTICLES

Ackrill, J.L. 'Aristotle on Eudaimonia', *Proceedings of the British Academy*, 60, 1974: 339–59 in Rorty (1980)
Annas, J. 'Plato and Aristotle on Friendship and Altruism', *Mind*, 86 (1977): 532–54
——'Aristotle on Pleasure and Goodness' in Rorty (1980): 285–99
Barnes, J 'Aristotle and the Methods of Ethics', *Revue Internationale de Philosophie* 34 (1980): 490–511
Burnyeat, M. F. 'Aristotle on Learning to be Good' in Rorty (1980)
Cooper, J.M. 'Aristotle on Friendship' in Rorty (1980): 301–4
Curzer, H. 'Aristotle's Much Maligned Megalopsychos' *Australasian Journal of Philosophy*, 69 (1991): 131–151
——'Aristotle's Bad Advice About Becoming Good in NE II' *Philosophy*, 71 (1996): 139–146.
Finley, M.I. 'Aristotle and Economic Analysis' in Barnes *et al* (1977)
Glassen, P. 'A Fallacy in Aristotle's Argument about the Good' *The Philosophical Quarterly*, 7 (1957): 319–22
Irwin, T.H. 'Reason and Responsibility in Aristotle' in Rorty (1980)
——'Permanent Happiness: Aristotle and Solon' in Sherman (1999)
Kenny, A. 'Aristotle on Happiness' *Proceedings of the Aristotelian Society* (1965–6): 93–102
Kraut, R. 'Two Conceptions of Happiness' *Philosophical Review* 88 (1979): 167–197
McDowell, J. 'The Role of Eudaimonia in Aristotle's Ethics', in Rorty (1980): 359–376
Molin, J. 'Contemplation and the Human Good' in *Nous* (1983)
Nagel, T. 'Aristotle on Eudaimonia' in Rorty (1980)
Owen, G.E.L. 'Aristotelian Pleasures' *Proceedings of Aristotelian Society* 72 (1971–2): 135–152
Pears, D. 'Courage as a Mean' in Rorty (1980): 171–88

Robinson, R 'Aristotle on Akrasia' in his *Essays in Greek Philosophy* (Oxford: Oxford University Press, 1969)

Rorty, A.O. 'Akrasia and Pleasure: Nicomachean Ethics Book 7' in Rorty (1980)

Sorabji, R. 'Aristotle on the Role of Intellect in Virtue' in Rorty (1980)

Urmson, J.O. 'Aristotle's Doctrine of the Mean' in Rorty (1980)

Whiting, J. 'Aristotle's Function Argument: A Defence' in ed. T. Irwin *Classical Philosophy vol. 5: Aristotle's Ethics* (NY, 1995)

Wiggins, D. 'Deliberation and Practical Reason' *Proceedings of the Aristotelian Society* 76 (1975–76): 29–51 reprinted in Rorty (1980)

'Weakness of Will, Commensurability and the Objects of Deliberation and Desire' *Proceedings of the Aristotelian Society*, 79 (1978–79): 251–277 reprinted in Rorty (1980)

Wilkes, K.V. 'The Good Man and the Good for Man' in Rorty (1980)

Williams, B. 'A Formal Sketch of Aristotle's Argument for the Good' *The Philosophical Quarterly* 12 (1962): 289–296

——'Justice as a Virtue' in Rorty (1980)

5. WORKS OTHERWISE REFERRED TO

Adkins, A.W.H. *Merit and Responsibility* (Oxford: Clarendon Press, 1960)

Annas, J. *The Morality of Happiness* (Oxford: Oxford University Press, 1993)

Anscombe 'Modern Moral Philosophy' in Crisp, R. & Slote, M. (1997)

Aquinas *Summa Theologiae* (New York: Hafner Publishing, 1953)

Argyle, M. *The Psychology of Happiness* (London: Routledge, 1987)

Athanassoulis, N. 'A Response to Harman: Virtue Ethics and Character Traits' *Proceedings of the Aristotelian Society*, 100 (2000): 215–221

Barnes, J. 'Introduction' in Thomson (1955)

Burke, E. *An Inquiry into our Ideas of the Beautiful and Sublime* (Oxford: Oxford University Press, 1990)

Butler, J. *Five Sermons* (Indianapolis: Hackett, 1983)

Crisp, R. & Slote, M. *Virtue Ethics* (Oxford: Oxford University Press, 1997)

Davidson, D. 'How Weakness of Will is Possible' in *Essays on Actions and Events* (Oxford: Oxford University Press, 1980)

Dent, N.J.H. *The Moral Psychology of the Virtues* (Cambridge: Cambridge University Press, 1984)

——*Rousseau: An Introduction to his Psychological, Social and Political Theory* (Oxford: Blackwell, 1988)

Foot, P. *Natural Goodness* (Oxford: Oxford University Press, 2001)

Goldie, P. *On Personality* (New York: Routledge, 2004)

Hampshire, S. *Two Theories of Morality* (Oxford: Clarendon Press, 1977)

Harman, G. 'Moral philosophy meets social psychology' *Proceedings of Aristotelian Society* 99 (1999): 315–331

Hobbes, T. *Leviathan* (London: Penguin, 1651 [1985])

Holton, R. 'How Strength of Will is Possible' in S. Stroud and C. Tappolet eds. *Weakness of Will and Practical Irrationality* (Oxford: Clarendon Press, 2003) pp. 39–67

Hume, D. *A Treatise on Human Nature* (Oxford: Clarendon Press, 1978)
Hume, D. *An Enquiry Concerning the Principles of Morals* (Indianapolis: Hackett, 1751 [1983])
Hursthouse, R. *On Virtue Ethics* (Oxford: Oxford University Press, 1999)
Huysmans, A.E. *Against Nature* (London: Penguin, 1884 [1959])
Kant, I. *The Moral Law* trans. H. Paton (London: Hutchinson, 1785 [1948])
——*The Metaphysic of Morals* trans. M. Gregor (New York: Cambridge University Press, 1996)
——*Critique of Judgement* trans. J.C. Meredith (Oxford: Oxford University Press, 1790 [1988])
MacIntyre, A. *A Short History of Ethics* (London: Routledge, 1967 [1998])
——*After Virtue* (London: Duckworth 1981 [1985])
Matthews, G 'Weakness of Will' *Mind* 75 (1966): 405–19
Mill, J.S. 'Utilitarianism' in *On Liberty and Other Essays* (Oxford: Oxford University Press, 1861 [1991])
Montaigne, M. *Essays* (London: Penguin, 1958)
Plato *Early Socratic Dialogues* (London: Penguin 1987)
——*Protagoras and Meno* (London: Penguin, 1956)
——*Republic* (London: Penguin, 1955)
Rawls, J. *A Theory of Justice* (Oxford: Oxford University Press, 1971)
Rousseau, J-J. *The Reveries of a Solitary Walker* trans. P. Walker (London: Penguin, 1979)
Russell, B. *The Conquest of Happiness* (London: Routledge, 1930 [2003])
Schopenhauer, A. *The World as Will and Representation* 2 vols. (Dover, 1819, 1844 [1961])
——*Essays and Aphorisms* (London: Penguin, 1970 [1851])
Scruton, R. *Sexual Desire* (London: Weidenfeld & Nicolson, 1985)
Theophrastus *Characters* (Cambridge, MA: Loeb, 2002)
Veblen, T. *The Theory of the Leisure Class* (Dover, 1899 [1991])
Von Wright, G.H. *The Varieties of Goodness* (London: Routledge, 1963)
Williams, B. *Ethics and the Limits of Philosophy* (London: Fontana, 1985)
Wollheim, R. *The Thread of Life* (New Haven: Yale, 1985)

INDEX